STATS

MATH MADE FUN!

by

Don Fraser

SOMERVILLE HOUSE, USA
NEW YORK

Copyright © 1999 Somerville House Books Limited
and NHL Enterprises, L.P.

ISBN: 1-58184-033-0   A B C D E F G H I J

Printed in Canada

Writer: Don Fraser
Designer: FiWired.com

Photographs
cover: Rick Stewart/Allsport
page 13: top left, Jim McIsaac/Bruce Bennett Studios;
top right, Jim McIsaac/Bruce Bennett Studios;
2nd row, left, M.Buckner/Bruce Bennett Studios;
2nd row, right, Jim McIsaac/Bruce Bennett Studios;
3rd row, left, B. Bennett/Bruce Bennett Studios;
3rd row, right, J. Russell/Bruce Bennett Studios;
bottom row, left, Jim McIsaac/Bruce Bennett Studios;
bottom row, right, J. Giamundo/Bruce Bennett Studios;
page 26-27: C. Anderson/Bruce Bennett Studios

Somerville House, USA is distributed by
Penguin Putnam Books for Young Readers,
345 Hudson Street, New York, N.Y. 10014

Published in Canada by Somerville House Publishing
a division of Somerville House Books Limited
3080 Yonge Street, Suite 5000
Toronto, ON
M4N 3N1

e-mail: sombooks@goodmedia.com
Web site: www.sombooks.com

Contents

The NHL Teams

How well do you know the teams in the National Hockey League?

The teams and home bases are all mixed up. Show how well you know the NHL by joining the teams and home bases correctly.

EASTERN CONFERENCE

NORTHEAST DIVSION

Boston	Sabres
Buffalo	Canadiens
Montreal	Maple Leafs
Ottawa	Bruins
Toronto	Senators

ATLANTIC DIVSION

New Jersey	Penguins
New York	Flyers
Philadelphia	Rangers
New York	Devils
Pittsburgh	Islanders

SOUTHEAST DIVSION

Carolina	Panthers
Florida	Lightning
Tampa Bay	Thrashers
Washington	Capitals
Atlanta	Hurricanes

WESTERN CONFERENCE

CENTRAL DIVSION

Chicago	Red Wings
Detroit	Blackhawks
Nashville	Blues
Columbus	Predators
St. Louis	Blue Jackets

NORTHWEST DIVSION

Calgary	Canucks
Colorado	Avalanche
Edmonton	Oilers
Minnesota	Wild
Vancouver	Flames

PACIFIC DIVSION

Anaheim	Kings
Dallas	Sharks
Los Angeles	Stars
Phoenix	Mighty Ducks
San Jose	Coyotes

ARE YOU SERIOUS ?

In the 1990s 7 teams entered the NHL:

1991   San Jose

1992   Ottawa, Tampa Bay

1993   Anaheim, Florida

1998   Nashville

1999   Atlanta

Around The World

NHL players now expect to have teammates from around the world.

*"It's not a big deal anymore.
There's six different languages flying
around our dressing room alone."*

- Ottawa Senators Defenseman, **Wade Redden**

In the 1999 NHL All-Star Game in Tampa, players born in 10 different countries competed. The players were born in Canada, United States, Czech Republic, Latvia, Russia, Sweden, Germany, Finland, Slovakia, and the Ukraine.

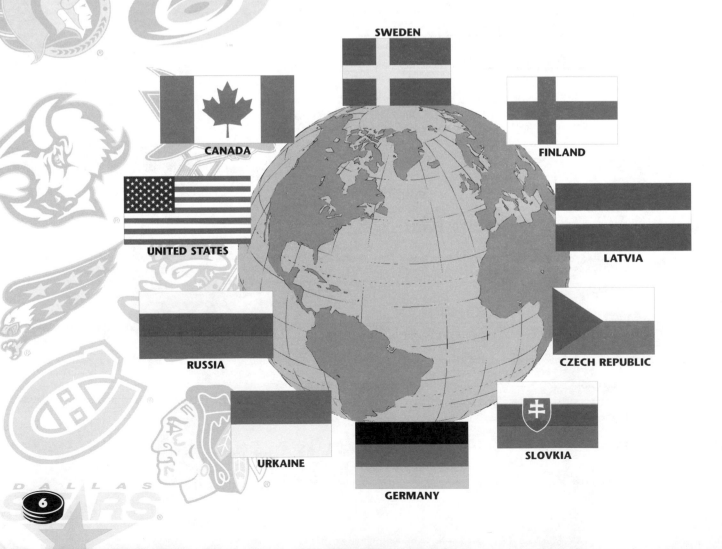

SWEDEN

CANADA

FINLAND

UNITED STATES

LATVIA

RUSSIA

CZECH REPUBLIC

URKAINE

SLOVKIA

GERMANY

This chart shows the number of players born in each country for five NHL teams in 1999.

COUNTRY	Philadelphia	Detroit	Colorado	New Jersey	Dallas	TOTAL
Canada	14	15	14	11	12	
United States	2	1	4	6	5	
Sweden	1	3	1	0	0	
Czech Republic	1	0	1	3	1	
Russia	4	3	2	2	1	12
Finland	0	0	0	0	1	
Germany	0	1	0	0	0	
Latvia	0	0	1	0	0	
Poland	0	0	0	1	0	
TOTAL	22					

Find the missing totals in the chart by adding.

CALCULATOR CORNER

What percent of the players were born in Canada? _____%

What percent of the players were born in the United States? _____%

What percent of the players were born in Europe? _____%

You Can't Tell The Players Without A Program

These are the numbers worn by many hockey stars:

1	Damian Rhodes
2	Al MacInnis
3	Curtis Joseph
4	Rob Blake
5	Nicklas Lidstrom
6	Wade Redden
7	Keith Tkachuk
8	Teemu Selanne
9	Paul Kariya
10	John LeClair
11	Mark Messier
12	Peter Bondra
13	Mats Sundin
14	Theoren Fleury
16	Bobby Holik
17	Rod Brind'Amour
19	Alexei Yashin
20	Ed Belfour
21	Peter Forsberg
22	Roman Hamrlik
24	Niklas Sundstrom
25	Vincent Damphousse
27	Teppo Numminen
30	Martin Brodeur
33	Patrick Roy
39	Dominik Hasek
44	Chris Pronger
55	Keith Primeau
68	Jaromir Jagr
77	Ray Bourque
88	Eric Lindros
91	Sergei Fedorov
97	Jeremy Roenick
99	Wayne Gretzky

To answer the questions on this page:
- **A.** Replace the player by his number on the opposite page.
- **B.** Do the arithmetic.
- **C.** Replace the number answer by a player name.

> *e.g.* LeClair + Kariya
> = 10 + 9
> = 19
> = Yashin

From the hockey stars list on the opposite page, make up your own questions similar to the ones you have answered. Without showing the answers, have a friend try to answer the questions. See who can make the longest true equation.

Assign player numbers to everybody in your class. Using this new list of names and numbers, make up some player number questions for a friend to try.

1. Lidstrom + Tkachuk = _____

2. Holik + Brind'Amour = _____

3. Pronger – Brodeur = _____

4. Sundstrom – Yashin = _____

5. Hamrlik + Primeau = _____

6. Fedorov – Bourque =

_____

7. Numminen – Selanne = _____

8. Redden + Bondra + Forsberg = _____

9. Joseph + LeClair - Tkachuk + Fleury =

_____

10. Try to find five answers for this question:

_____ + _____ = Gretzky

_____ + _____ = Gretzky

_____ + _____ = Gretzky

_____ + _____ = Gretzky

_____ + _____ = Gretzky

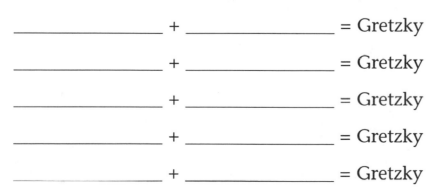

Happy Birthday!

Let's explore the patterns in birthdays with two of hockey's best teams — Dallas Stars and Philadelphia Flyers.

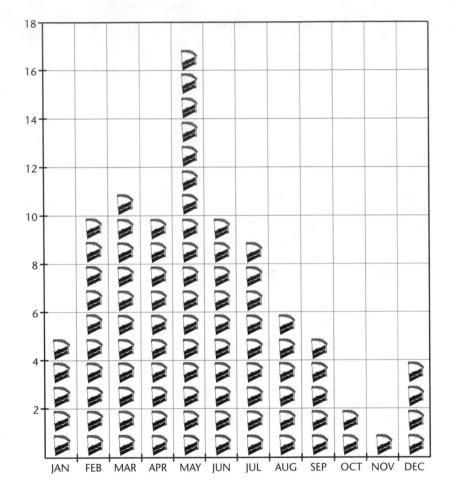

1. In which month were most players born?

   _____

2. How many players were born in the first half of the year? _____
   In the second half of the year? _____

   Can you think of a reason why the difference between these two answers is so great?

   _____

NHL All-Stars seem to be born in each month of the year. Here's a sample:

Dominik Hasek	January 29, 1965
Jaromir Jagr	February 15, 1972
Pavel Bure	March 31, 1971
Curtis Joseph	April 29, 1967
Steve Yzerman	May 9, 1965
Theoren Fleury	June 29, 1968
Peter Forsberg	July 20, 1973
Brett Hull	August 9, 1964
Martin Straka	September 3, 1972
Paul Kariya	October 16, 1974
Keith Primeau	November 24, 1971
Rob Blake	December 10, 1969

3. How old was Pavel Bure in 1999? _____

4. Who is older, Peter Forsberg or Jaromir Jagr?

    _____

5. Who is the youngest player on the list?

    _____

    How old was he in 1999? _____

6. Who is the oldest player? _____
    How old was he in 1999? _____

OVERTIME

00:00

What is the month and day of your birthday?
Month _____
Day _____

Which hockey star's birthday is closest to yours?
_____

How close?
_____

Birthday Matches

Did you know that Teemu Selanne and Teppo Numminen were born in Finland? They also have matching birthdays. They were born on the same day — July 3!

This graph tells us that in any group of 24 people, the chance of at least one pair of matching birthdays is about 50%. This is about the same chance of getting "heads" when you flip a coin.

THE CHANCE OF A BIRTHDAY MATCH

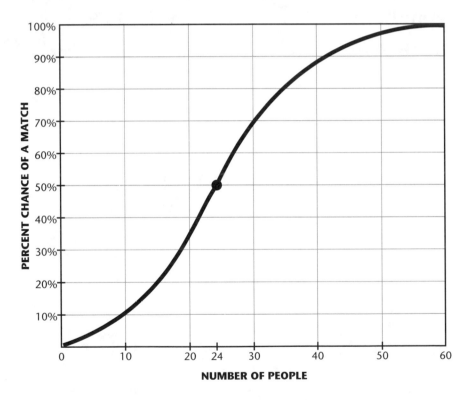

Using the graph, approximately what are the chances of a birthday match in a group of:

50 people? _____   40 people? _____

30 people? _____   20 people? _____

10 people? _____

There are a number of other birthday matches in the NHL:

Eric Lindros and **Shawn McEachern**
February 28

Roman Hamrlik and **Adam Graves**
April 12

Alexei Zhitnik and **Chris Pronger**
October 10

Ray Bourque and **Rob Niedermayer**
December 28

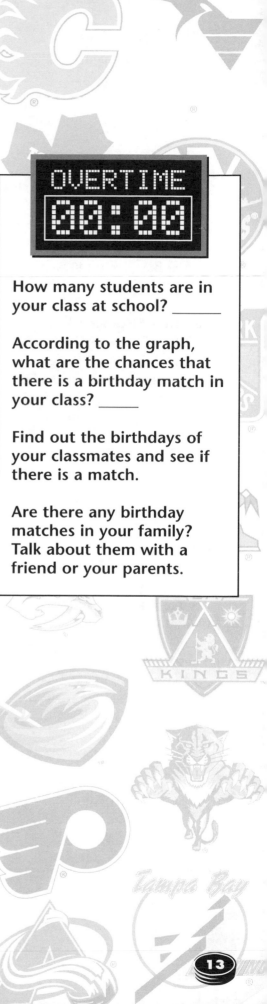

OVERTIME
00:00

How many students are in your class at school? _____

According to the graph, what are the chances that there is a birthday match in your class? _____

Find out the birthdays of your classmates and see if there is a match.

Are there any birthday matches in your family? Talk about them with a friend or your parents.

Score Search

Here are the scores from several NHL games during the 1998/99 season. In each game the visiting team is written first, the home team second. OT stands for overtime.

Friday, October 9
Philadelphia 1, N.Y. Rangers 0
Tampa Bay 1, Florida 4
San Jose 3, Calgary 3 OT

Saturday October 10
St. Louis 3, Boston 3
Detroit 1, Toronto 2
N.Y. Rangers 1, Montreal 7
Pittsburgh 4, N.Y. Islanders 3
Anaheim 0, Washington 1
Tampa Bay 4, Carolina 4 OT
New Jersey 1, Chicago 2
Florida 1, Nashville 0
Ottawa 4, Colorado 3
Los Angeles 2, Edmonton 1
Buffalo 1, Dallas 4
Calgary 5, San Jose 3

Sunday, October 11
Anaheim 1, Philadelphia 4
Ottawa 4, Phoenix 1

Tuesday, October 13
Anaheim 0, Montreal 1
Detroit 3, Washington 2
Carolina 2, Nashville 3
Toronto 3, Edmonton 2
Chicago 1, Dallas 3

Wednesday, October 14
Pittsburgh 3, New Jersey 1
N.Y. Islanders 2, Tampa Bay 0
Boston 3, Colorado 0
Edmonton 4, Vancouver 1

Thursday, November 12
Edmonton 1, Ottawa 1 OT
Montreal 0, N.Y. Islanders 4
Florida 2, Philadelphia 1
Buffalo 2, Washington 1
Toronto 10, Chicago 3
Vancouver 4, Calgary 3
Nashville 3, Los Angeles 1
Carolina 0, San Jose 3

Saturday, November 21
Washington 4, Boston 5 OT
Buffalo 1, Toronto 2
Colorado 3, Montreal 2
Calgary 1, Ottawa 4
Florida 3, New Jersey 3 OT
Tampa Bay 2, Pittsburgh 5
Dallas 3, St. Louis 3 OT
N.Y. Islanders 6, Nashville 3
Detroit 4, Vancouver 2
Edmonton 2, Phoenix 3 OT
Chicago 0, Los Angeles 5
N.Y. Rangers 2, San Jose 2 OT

Sunday, November 22
New Jersey 5, Carolina 2
Philadelphia 2, Florida 1 OT
Chicago 1, Anaheim 4

Monday, November 23
Calgary 2, Toronto 3
Vancouver 3, Ottawa 4
San Jose 2, Dallas 3

Thursday, December 10
New Jersey 5, Philadelphia 4 OT
Boston 3, Carolina 2
San Jose 1, Nashville 2

Friday, December 11
N.Y. Rangers 0, Buffalo 2
Calgary 2, Tampa Bay 1
Edmonton 2, Detroit 3
Toronto 3, Chicago 2
Montreal 2, Dallas 3
Washington 0, Anaheim 1

Monday, December 14
Phoenix 2, Montreal 2 OT
Calgary 2, N.Y. Rangers 5
St. Louis 0, Colorado 0 OT

Wednesday, December 16
Phoenix 2, Toronto 5
N.Y. Rangers 3, New Jersey 6
Pittsburgh 1, Florida 4
Boston 3, Detroit 5
Nashville 1, Anaheim 6

The answers to your searches are found somewhere on the opposite page.

Search 1
Find the number of overtime games on November 21. _____

Search 2
On what day was every score the same?

_____

Search 3
Find the highest scoring game.

_____

Search 4
Find the lowest scoring game.

_____

Search 5
Find the day when the visiting teams won every game. _____

Search 6
Find the days when the home team won every game. _____

Search 7
Find the days when there was exactly a one-goal difference between the teams in every game. _____

Search 8
Find the three days when there was more than a one-goal difference between the teams in every game. _____ _____ _____

Using the Game Summaries on pages **58 – 64** or using current newspapers, collect NHL scores for a number of days. With this new data try the eight searches again. Also look for new patterns in the scores and create a different search!

Goals + Assists = Points

Most hockey players are very interested in the formula

"goals + assists = points" or "g + a = p."

This means that each goal a player scores counts as 1 point. Each assist a player receives for helping a teammate score also counts as 1 point.

For example, on February 7, 1976 Darryl Sittler set a record for most points in one game when he had 6 goals and 4 assists for a total of 10 points!

In alphabetical order in this chart are the top 10 point-getters for 1997/98.

Player	Goals	Assists	Points
Allison, Jason	33	50	
Bure, Pavel	51	39	
Forsberg, Peter	25	66	
Francis, Ron	25	62	
Gretzky, Wayne	23	67	
Jagr, Jaromir	35	67	
LeClair, John	51	36	
Palffy, Zigmund	45	42	
Selanne, Teemu	52	34	
Stumpel, Jozef	21	58	

1. Complete the points column for each player.

2a. Who won the Art Ross Trophy awarded to the player with the most points for the season?

_____

b. Who was runner-up?

_____

3. Try to answer these questions without doing any adding! Estimation, number sense, and common sense will do the job. After getting the answers explain your reasoning.

a. In 1995/96 Joe Sakic scored 51 goals and 69 assists. Eric Lindros counted 47 goals and 68 assists.

Who had more points?

_____

b. That same season, Ron Francis had 27 goals and 92 assists. Mario Lemieux had 69 goals and 92 assists.

Who had more points?

_____

c. In 1996/97 Paul Kariya had 44 goals and 55 assists. Brendan Shanahan had 47 goals and 41 assists.

Who had more points?

_____

The GAP

The standard of excellence for individual high-scoring players is a "100-point" season. A player has a 100-point season if the total of his goals plus assists is greater than or equal to 100. This graph shows how frequently this happens.

OVERTIME

00:00

Can you guess why nobody reached 100 points in 1994/95?

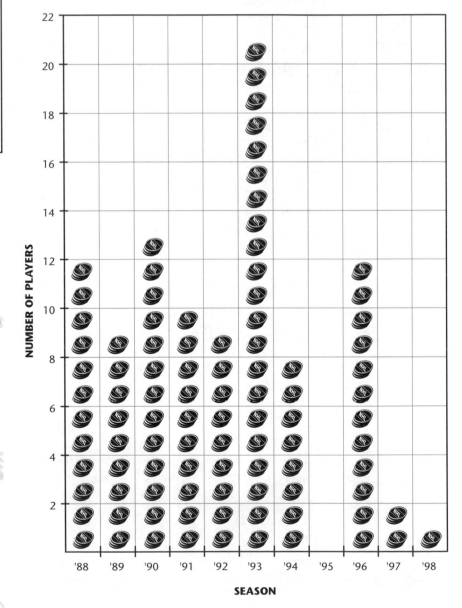

100-POINT SEASONS

NUMBER OF PLAYERS

SEASON

1. In the 1996/97 season only Mario Lemieux and Teemu Selanne had 100-point seasons. That season Paul Kariya had 44 goals.

What is the most number of assists that Kariya could have had? _____

2. A newspaper clipping revealed this information on February 15, 1999:

NHL LEADERS

	G	A	P
Jagr	26	55	81
Lindros	32	43	
LeClair	34		69
Kariya		44	67

Complete the stats missing from the newspaper clipping.

3. Find out more about Alexei Yashin's accomplishments during 1996/97 and 1997/98:

During the two seasons Yashin totaled 147 points.

In the first season he had 35 goals and 40 assists.

In the second season he earned 39 assists.

How many goals did Alexei Yashin score in the second season? _____

Great Goal Scorers

Nobody has scored more goals in the NHL than Wayne Gretzky!

For example, in 1980/81 he potted a record shattering 92 goals. The next three seasons he followed up with 71, 87, and 73 goals.

Gretzky also led the NHL in goal scoring a fifth time in 1986/87 with 62 goals.

In this graph, let's find out about the top goal scorers since then.

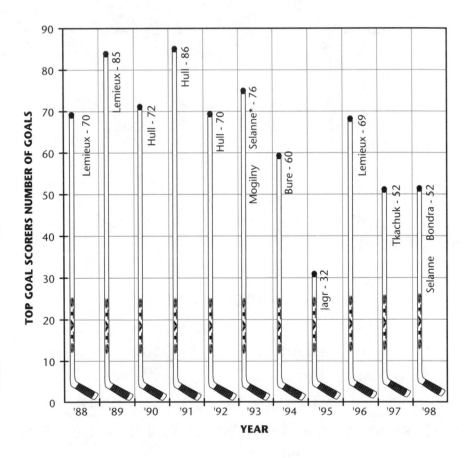

* In 1992/93 Teemu Selanne was a 22-year-old rookie!

1. After Wayne Gretzky's 92-goal season, which two players have scored the most goals in a season? How many did they score?

   _____   ___

   _____   ___

2. Since Gretzky, who is the only player to lead the NHL in goal scoring three years in a row?

   _____

3. Theoren Fleury has shown that size doesn't always matter in hockey! Although only 5' 6" (165 cm) tall, Fleury never backs down from the bigger players and is a wonderful goal scorer. As a rookie Fleury scored 31 goals. In his next season he scored 51 goals.

   How many goals did Fleury score over his first two seasons? _____

4. In his first three seasons in Philadelphia, after being traded from the Montreal Canadiens, John LeClair scored 152 goals.

   LeClair scored the same number of goals in the first and third seasons and 50 goals in the middle season.

   How many goals did he score in the first season? _____

5. A player scores a "hat trick" when he scores three goals in a game. In 1997/98 Keith Tkachuk, Pavel Bure, and Teemu Selanne each scored a hat trick three times! As we know from the graph, Selanne scored 52 goals that season. Bure scored one less goal than Selanne, but 11 more goals than Tkachuk.

   How many goals did Keith Tkachuk score?

CALCULATOR CORNER

During the 1997/98 season, there were 64 games in which a player scored at least three goals in one game. Given that there were 26 teams, each playing in 82 games, would you expect to see a hat trick about once every:

A) 64 games
B) 8 games
C) 16 games
D) 2132 games

ARE YOU SERIOUS ?

On March 23, 1952 Bill Mosienko scored three goals within 21 seconds!

Points Puzzlers

Mario Lemieux is the only player in NHL history to average over 2 points per game in his career! The *NHL Guide and Record Book* says that he averaged 2.005 points per game.

To find this number, divide his points (P) by the number of games he played (GP). Then express the answer correct to 3 decimal places.

$$1495 \div 745 = 2.005$$

1a. In an unbelievable eleven seasons, Wayne Gretzky led the NHL in point scoring. Eight of these league-leading seasons were in a row from 1980 to 1987.

Use a calculator to help you find his points per game (PPG) in each of these seasons:

SEASON	P	GP	PPG
1979/80	137	79	_____
1980/81	164	80	_____
1981/82	212	80	_____
1982/83	196	80	_____
1983/84	205	74	_____
1984/85	208	80	_____
1985/86	215	80	_____
1986/87	183	79	_____

b. In which season did Gretzky have the most points? _____

c. In which season did Gretzky have his best points per game average? _____

For these problems put away your calculator and your pencil and paper. By using your number sense, common sense, and mental math, you'll be able to answer these questions!

In the playoffs

2. The NHL record for most goals in the playoffs was set by Reggie Leach in 1976 with the Flyers and Jari Kurri in 1985 with the Oilers.

   Leach had 19 goals in 16 games. Kurri had 19 goals in 18 games.

   Which player had the better goals-per-game average? _____

3. The table on the right lists the six years in the playoffs Wayne Gretzky had the most points:

   a. Compare 1983 and 1987. In which year did Gretzky have the better points-per-game average? _____

   b. Compare 1984 and 1988. Which was the better points-per-game year for Gretzky? _____ Why? _____

Gretzky Leads all Playoff Scorers		
SEASON	P	GP
1983	38	16
1984	35	19
1985	47	18
1987	34	21
1988	43	19
1993	40	24

4. Check the table on the right for the point-scoring leaders in the playoffs. Each player was either on the Stanley Cup winner or on the team that lost in the final playoff series.

   Without doing the calculations, but using number sense, explain why each player had a better points-per-game record than Steve Yzerman.

Other Playoff Leading Scorers			
YEAR	PLAYER	P	GP
1998	Yzerman	24	22
1997	Lindros	26	19
1996	Sakic	34	22
1995	Fedorov	24	17
1994	Leetch	34	23

Close Games

Make a guess! Circle one of these answers:

The difference in goals between the winning team and the losing team is most often:

A. 1 goal **B.** 2 goals **C.** 3 goals
D. 4 goals **E.** 5 or more goals

1. Complete this chart of scores of NHL games by finding the "difference" in goals between the teams in each game. This is often called "the winning margin."

Visiting Team		Home Team		Difference
Florida	2	N.Y. Islanders	6	4
Colorado	3	Carolina	2	
Vancouver	3	Edmonton	5	
Boston	2	Buffalo	4	
N.Y. Rangers	1	New Jersey	3	
Philadelphia	4	Pittsburgh	4	
Calgary	5	Detroit	2	
Colorado	0	Toronto	3	
Montreal	4	N.Y. Rangers	1	
Tampa Bay	5	Washington	2	
Chicago	1	Florida	2	
Nashville	2	Edmonton	3	
St. Louis	3	Anaheim	1	
Dallas	0	San Jose	4	
Toronto	1	Boston	4	
Pittsburgh	4	Ottawa	2	
Carolina	6	N.Y. Islanders	3	
St. Louis	2	L. A.	2	
Carolina	3	Washington	2	
Chicago	2	Tampa Bay	2	
Nashville	2	Calgary	1	
Colorado	5	Edmonton	2	
Detroit	1	Phoenix	3	

2. Use the differences you have calculated to complete this graph. The first column is done for you.

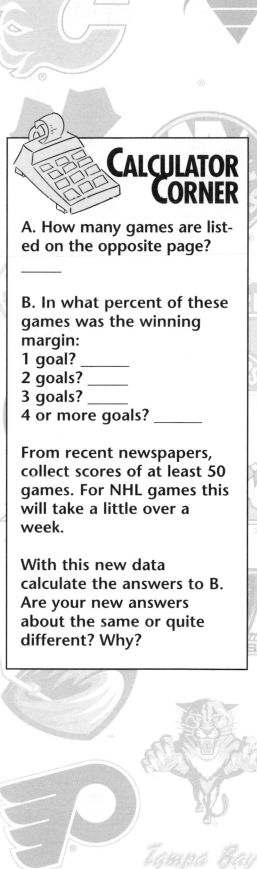

THE NUMBERS OF GOALS A TEAM WINS BY

(y-axis) NUMBER OF GAMES

CALCULATOR CORNER

A. How many games are listed on the opposite page?

_____

B. In what percent of these games was the winning margin:
1 goal? _____
2 goals? _____
3 goals? _____
4 or more goals? _____

From recent newspapers, collect scores of at least 50 games. For NHL games this will take a little over a week.

With this new data calculate the answers to B. Are your new answers about the same or quite different? Why?

3. According to the graph what is the answer to the multiple choice question at the top of the previous page?

Home Team

In any NHL game one team is the "visiting" "team," the other is the "home team."

What are some advantages to being the home team? Does the visiting team have any advantages? Talk this over with a friend.

Would you prefer to be on the visiting team or the home team? Why?

On February 20, 1999 the Toronto Maple Leafs played its first game in its new home, called the Air Canada Centre. Here are the results:

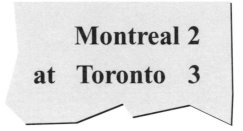

Montreal 2
at Toronto 3

The home team, Toronto, beat the visiting team, Montreal 3-2.

Air Canada Centre, Toronto, Canada

The following activity explores whether the home team wins most of the time!

1a. Using the 40 Game Summaries on pages 58-64 complete the chart at right. In the Winning Team column,
if the home team won the game, then fill in H.
If the visiting team won, fill in a V.
If the game was tied, write T.

b. How many games did the home team win? _____

How many games did the visiting team win? _____

How many games were tied? _____

c. Would you say the home team wins "most of the time"? Explain.

_____

Game Number	Winning Team
1	
2	
3	
4	
5	
6	
7	
8	
9	
10	
11	
12	
13	
14	
15	
16	
17	
18	
19	
20	
21	
22	
23	
24	
25	
26	
27	
28	
29	
30	
31	
32	
33	
34	
35	
36	
37	
38	
39	
40	

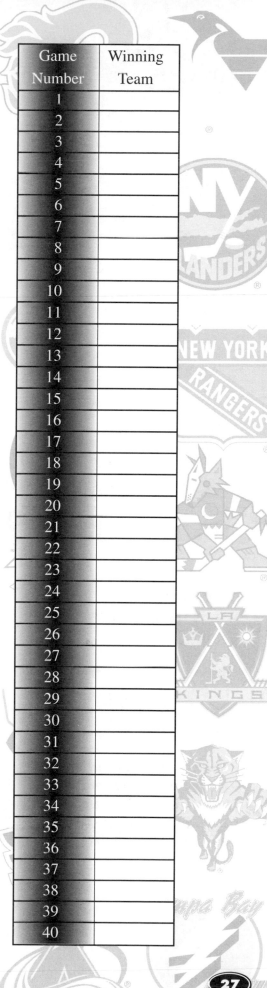

NHL Team Standings

In 1998/99 the NHL was made up of 26 teams divided into six divisions. Below are standings for one of those divisions partway through the season.

NHL STANDINGS
EASTERN CONFERENCE
Northeast Division

	GP	W	L	T
Toronto	46	27	16	3
Ottawa	45	25	14	6
Buffalo	43	23	13	7
Boston	43	20	16	7
Montreal	46	17	21	8

This chart tells us that Toronto has played 46 games — winning 27, losing 16, and tying 3.

Use the NHL Standings to help you answer these questions:

1. How many games has Buffalo played? _____

2. How many games has Boston lost? _____

3. How many games has Ottawa tied? _____

4. Which team has won the most games?

____

ARE YOU SERIOUS?

Most wins:
In 1995/96 Detroit Red Wings won 62 of its 82 games.

Longest winning streak:
In 1993 Pittsburgh Penguins won 17 games in a row.

Longest undefeated streak:
In 1992/93 Philadelphia Flyers played 35 games in a row before losing. They won 25 and tied 10.

Since a team either wins or loses or ties a game, we have this formula:

Games Played = Wins + Losses + Ties

or

GP = W + L + T

5. Use this formula and number sense to complete the Team Standings:

NHL STANDINGS
WESTERN CONFERENCE
Pacific Division

	GP	W	L	T
Dallas		27	9	7
Phoenix		24	11	7
Anaheim	45		19	9
San Jose	45	15		12
Los Angeles	45	16	25	

6. In 1998/99 each team played an 82-game schedule. Years ago teams played a different number of games.

a. The NHL started in 1917/18 with four teams. That year the Montreal Canadiens won 13 games, lost 9, and did not tie.

How many games did the Canadiens play?

_____

b. In 1924/25 the Boston Bruins were the first American team in the NHL. They won 6 games, did not tie, and lost 24 games.

How many games did the Bruins play?

_____

c. 1993/94 was a long regular season! Vancouver Canucks won 46 games, lost 29, and tied 9 games.

How many games did Vancouver play?

_____

A Winning Formula

A team's points are based on the following formula:

Two points for each win
One point for each tie
Zero points for each loss

Mathematicians would write this formula as:

Pts = 2 x W + T

For example, in 1997/98 New Jersey Devils earned the most points in the NHL.

The Devils won 48 games, lost 23 games, and tied 11 games.

The Devils had 2 x 48 + 11 = 107 points.

1. There were 13 teams in the Eastern Conference in 1996/97. The eight teams with the most points qualified for the playoffs.

   Calculate the points each team had and circle the teams that went on to the playoffs:

	W	L	T	Pts
Boston	26	47	9	_____
Buffalo	40	30	12	_____
Florida	35	28	19	_____
Hartford	32	39	11	_____
Montreal	31	36	15	_____
New Jersey	45	23	14	_____
New York Islanders	29	41	12	_____
New York Rangers	38	34	10	_____
Ottawa	31	36	15	_____
Philadelphia	45	24	13	_____
Pittsburgh	38	36	8	_____
Tampa Bay	32	40	10	_____
Washington	33	40	9	_____

Shoot to Win!

To qualify for the NHL® Open Net Sweepstakes, complete the reverse of this entry form and mail it to the address below, and you could be chosen as a lucky winner!

Mail all completed entry forms to:
Penguin Putnam Books for Young Readers
NHL® Open Net Sweepstakes
345 Hudson Street, New York, NY 10014

The Prizes
The Grand Prize Winner receives air travel (coach) for him/herself and a parent or guardian, hotel accommodations in Toronto, Canada for 2 nights (based on double occupancy) and tickets to the 2000 NHL® Award Ceremony. In addition, the winner will have his/her photo taken with an NHL star, tour the arena, and other VIP treatment. Grand prize includes $350 (U.S.) stipend for meals, taxis and incidentals on the trip. (No other expenses are included. Winner and companion are responsible for transportation to and from the airport. Reservations once made may not be changed. Approximate retail value of grand prize ($2,255 U.S.) varies depending on point of departure in the United States.) Fifty Runners Up will receive a genuine NHL autographed hockey stick. (Approximate retail value is $75 U.S. per stick.)

How to Enter and Eligibility
NO PURCHASE NECESSARY. Enter by completing the official entry form (or by printing your name, address, age and phone number on a 3x5 card) and sending it in a business sized envelope to NHL® Open Net Sweepstakes, Penguin Putnam Inc., 345 Hudson Street, New York, NY 10014. No faxed entries will be accepted. Only one entry per envelope is permitted. Contest begins September 13, 1999. Entries must be received by January 1, 2000.

All contestants must be legal U.S. residents between the ages of 5 and 14 on January 1, 2000. Employees (and their families) of NHL Enterprises, L.P., NHL Enterprises, Canada, L.P., NHL Enterprises, B.V., the member clubs of the NHL (collectively the "NHL Entities"), Somerville House, USA and their respective affiliates, agencies, retailers, distributors, and advertising agencies, are not eligible to enter.

Official Rules
Winners will be selected the week of February 1, 2000 by a random drawing from all complete entries. Winners will be notified by mail on or around March 1, 2000. Odds of winning depend on number of entries received. Neither the NHL Entities nor Somerville House, USA is responsible for illegible entries or lost or misdirected mail. All entries become the property of Somerville House, USA and will not be returned. In the event there is an insufficient number of entries, Somerville House, USA reserves the right not to award all prizes. Judges decisions are final. Winners and their parents/legal guardians will be required to execute an affidavit of eligibility, a liability release, a publicity release and any other documentation that Somerville House, USA or NHL Entities require which must be returned within 14 days of notification or an alternative winner will be selected. Winners consent to the use of their name and/or photos or likeness for advertising and promotional purposes without additional compensation (except where prohibited). Taxes and fees are the sole responsibility of winners. Prizes cannot be transferred, redeemed for cash, or exchanged. Void where prohibited by law. All entrants are subject to, agree to comply with, and be bound by these rules. The NHL Entities, Somerville House, USA and their affiliates, officers, directors, employees, and agents shall not be liable for any claims related to this contest or any prize awarded. For the names of the winners, send a self-addressed stamped envelope to : NHL® Open Net Sweepstakes Winners, c/o Penguin Putnam Inc., 345 Hudson Street, New York, NY 10014.

2. The President's Trophy is awarded each season to the team with the most points. In 1996/97 Dallas won 48 games, lost 26, and tied 8. Colorado won 49 games, lost 24, and tied 9.

Without using paper and pencil, decide who won the trophy. _____

3a. Detroit Red Wings have 64 points. This is based on 30 wins and a certain number of ties.

How many ties does Detroit have? _____

b. Edmonton Oilers have 52 points. They have 8 ties and a certain number of wins.

How many games have Edmonton won? _____

c. San Jose Sharks have won 20 games and tied 13 games. Anaheim Mighty Ducks have won 3 more games than San Jose, but tied 4 fewer than San Jose.

How many points does Anaheim have? _____

d. Nashville Predators have 19 wins and 5 ties. St. Louis Blues have 3 more wins and 4 more ties than Nashville.

How many points does St. Louis have? _____

To solve these problems you will need to recall two formulas:

$$GP = W + L + T \quad \text{and} \quad Pts = 2 \times W + T$$

e. Toronto have played 55 games, losing 20 and tying 4.

How many wins does Toronto have? _____
How many points? _____

f. Carolina Hurricanes have 59 points. They have lost 22 games and tied 9.

How many games have Carolina played? _____

g. Phoenix Coyotes have played 54 games and have 68 points, including 10 ties.

How many games have Phoenix lost? _____

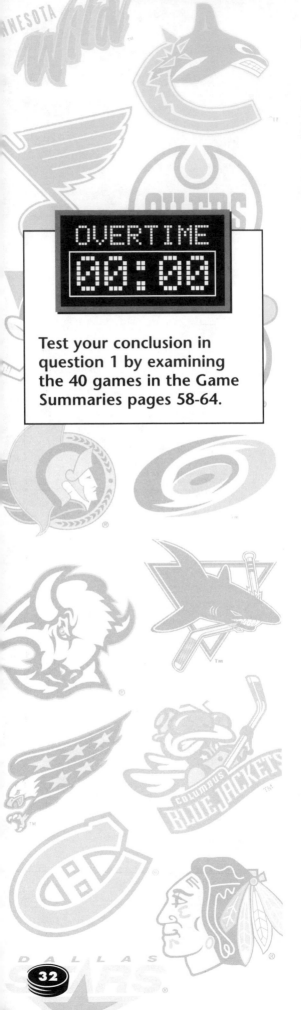

They Shoot, They Score

Statisticians keep track of a team's "shots-on-goal." A shot is considered a shot-on-goal, if and only if, it would have been a goal if the goalie or one of his teammates close to the goal hadn't stopped it. For example, a shot which hits the goalpost and bounces away, does not count as a shot-on-goal. However a goal is a shot-on-goal.

Test your conclusion in question 1 by examining the 40 games in the Game Summaries pages 58-64.

1. In a typical game how many shots-on-goal are there?

To help you answer this question, add up the shots-on-goal for each team in each period of these games. The first example is done for you.

a. Edmonton 10 8 13 |31|
Anaheim 8 13 11 |32|
Total |63|

b. Toronto 8 8 8 ☐
Washington 12 9 7 ☐
Total ☐

c. Phoenix 8 7 5 ☐
Pittsburgh 9 7 9 ☐
Total ☐

d. Carolina 16 14 8 ☐
Buffalo 12 8 16 ☐
Total ☐

e. Chicago 7 3 7 ☐
Dallas 11 13 7 ☐
Total ☐

f. Nashville 7 12 3 ☐
St. Louis 8 13 16 ☐
Total ☐

g. Tampa Bay 9 6 10 ☐
New Jersey 16 9 12 ☐
Total ☐

From your calculations, could you say that in a typical NHL game there is on average about one shot every minute? _____

2. By March in the 1998/99 NHL season some of the top goal scorers were

PLAYER	GOALS	GAMES	SHOTS
Theoren Fleury	30	60	250
John LeClair	38	60	185
Eric Lindros	36	58	198
Markus Naslund	31	59	153
Luc Robitaille	31	61	209
Teemu Selanne	34	54	194

Using estimation and mental math (no paper and pencil or calculator), about how many shots-on-goal do these great goal scorers have in a game? _____

3. In a game, does the winning team have more shots-on-goal?

To answer this question, use the Game Summaries on pages 58-64.

a. In how many of the 40 games was there a winning team? _____

b. In how many of the games in 3a did the winning team have more shots-on-goal?

_____

c. Does having more shots-on-goal seem to be an important factor in winning the game? Explain. _____

The First Goal Of A Game

How important is the first goal of a game? Does the team which scores the first goal of the game usually win?

1. The first goal of the game is described for each of these 7 NHL games.

   Circle the games in which the team that scored first won the game.

   (For more detail on how to read an NHL Game Summary see pages 52-53.)

Collect NHL Game Summaries from the newspaper over a number of days. From these Game Summaries explore the question at the top of page. Are your results similar to or different from the results in question 2? Why might this be?

Game A
Toronto **4**
at NY Islanders **1**
First Period
1. Toronto, Sundin 22
(Sullivan, Thomas), 19:33

Game B
Philadelphia **3**
at Washington **0**
First Period
1. Philadelphia, Lindros 23
(Desjardins, LeClair), 18:01

Game C
Chicago 2
at Ottawa 6
First Period
1. Ottawa, Yashin 25
(Dackell, Kravchuk), 3:01

Game D
Washington 3
at New Jersey 2
First Period
1. Washington, Bondra 26
(Oates), 3:54

Game E
NY Rangers 2
at Edmonton 1
First Period
No Scoring
Second Period
1. Edmonton, Grier 10
(Brown, McAmmond), 13:44

Game F
Los Angeles 1
at St. Louis 5
First Period
1. St. Louis, Demitra 26
(Picard, Helmer), 5:23

Game G
New Jersey 3
at Boston 3
First Period
1. New Jersey, Rolston 18
(Carpenter, Niedermayer), 16:49

Name _____

Age _____ phone # (optional) _____

Address _____

City _____

State _____ Zip Code _____

Entries must be received by January 1, 2000. Winners will be notified by mail on or about March 1, 2000

Mail all completed entry forms to:
Penguin Putnam Books for Young Readers
NHL® Open Net Sweepstakes
345 Hudson Street, New York, NY 10014

1

Grand
Prize Winner
will receive:
**a trip for 2
to the
2000 NHL®
Award Ceremony**

50

Runners-Up
will receive:
**a genuine
NHL®
autographed
hockey stick**

2. To investigate in detail the importance of a game's first goal, collect data from the 40 NHL Game Summaries on pages 58-64.

To help you collect the data, for each game in the Game Summaries, circle the team that scored first and put a box around the team that won.

In how many of the 40 games did the team which scored first:

Win? ____ games

Lose? ____ games

Tie? ____ games

Total 40 games

_____

CALCULATOR CORNER

Once again, using the 40 NHL Game Summaries on pages 58-64:

In how many games did the home team score first?

_____

For each of these games only, how many times did the home team win?

_____

If the home team scored first, in what percent of its games did the home team go on to win the game?

_____

If the home team scored first, in what percent of its games did the home team not lose?

_____

Updating The NHL Team Standings

In some newspapers the NHL Team Standings are presented in more detail than we have looked at so far.

GF stands for "goals for" — the number of goals the team has scored in all its games. GA stands for "goals against" — the number of goals opponents have scored against the team in all its games.

On February 21, 1999 the leading teams in each division were:

	GP	W	L	T	PTS	GF	GA
Philadelphia	57	30	14	13	73	178	122
Ottawa	56	32	16	8	72	164	118
Carolina	59	27	22	10	64	156	149
Detroit	59	31	23	5	67	175	147
Colorado	57	29	21	7	65	154	139
Dallas	54	35	10	9	79	159	107

READING THE STANDINGS

1. How many goals has Ottawa scored? _____

2. How many goals were scored against Detroit? _____

3. Which team has the fewest goals scored against it? _____

4. The answer is "Philadelphia, 178." What is the question?_____

In its next game Philadelphia lost, 5-3. Note how we update Philadelphia's record.

	GP	W	L	T	PTS	GF	GA
Philadelphia	58	30	15	13	73	181	127

Here is how the teams in the Northwest Division of the Western Conference stood on Tuesday, February 16, 1999

	GP	W	L	T	PTS	GF	GA
Colorado	55	29	21	5	63	149	134
Edmonton	54	21	25	8	50	146	142
Calgary	55	19	28	8	46	137	161
Vancouver	55	18	30	7	43	141	173

The results for the next few games involving these teams were:

St. Louis 8, Vancouver 1
Dallas 4, Edmonton 1
Chicago 4, Vancouver 0
Edmonton 6, Anaheim 2
Los Angeles 3, Edmonton 2
Colorado 4, Nashville 4
Calgary 6, Anaheim 3
Calgary 2, Los Angeles 2
Anahcim 5, Vancouver 1

5. Take the above scores and update the Standings from February 16.

	GP	W	L	T	PTS	GF	GA
Colorado							
Edmonton							
Calgary							
Vancouver							

OVERTIME
00:00

In this question we take a fictional Team Standings and use clues, logic, and number sense to find the scores of six games:

	GP	W	L	T	GF	GA
Bulldogs	3	3	0	0	12	3
Seals	3	1	1	1	8	6
Tigers	3	0	1	2	3	6
Falcons	3	0	2	1	1	9

Clues: Each team has played each other team once. The Bulldogs have won each game by the same score.

Use the above information to find the scores of all six games.

Bulldogs ____   Seals ____
Bulldogs ____   Tigers ____
Bulldogs ____   Falcons ____
Falcons ____   Tigers ____
Seals ____   Falcons____
Seals ____   Tigers ____

What's The Probability?

When people say, "What is the probability of something happening," they often expect an answer expressed as a fraction or a percent.

The probability that an NHL hockey game will be completed in 55 minutes is 0%. There is "no way" this can happen because each game has at least three 20-minute periods.

The probability that a team picks up two points for a win and one point for a tie in the NHL is a "sure thing" — 100%, because it's in the rule book.

Most probabilities lie somewhere between 0% and 100%! For example, flipping a coin and getting a head has a 50% probability.

On the opposite page are three investigations which start out asking, "What is the probability?" After guessing at the probability, collect data from the Game Summaries on pages 58-64 to help you calculate the probability.
(For more detail on how to read an NHL Game Summary see pages 52-53.)

1. Forgetting overtime, what is the probability that in an NHL game there will be penalties in every period?   My guess _____%

   From the Game Summaries
   a. The number of games considered _____
   b. The number of games where penalties were given in every period _____
   c. Divide b by a to calculate the probability _____%

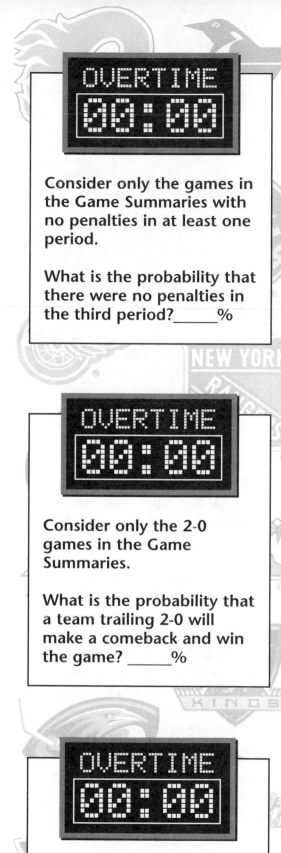

Consider only the games in the Game Summaries with no penalties in at least one period.

What is the probability that there were no penalties in the third period?_____%

2. After the first two goals of a game, the score must be 2-0 or 1-1.

   What is the probability in an NHL game that after two goals are scored the score is 2-0, rather than 1-1? My guess _____%

   From the Game Summaries
   a. The number of 2-0 games _____
   b. The number of 1-1 games _____
   c. Total number of games considered? _____
   d. Divide a by c to calculate the probability _____%

Consider only the 2-0 games in the Game Summaries.

What is the probability that a team trailing 2-0 will make a comeback and win the game? _____%

3. What is the probability in an NHL game that a team, winning at the end of two periods, will continue and win the game?
   My guess _____%

   From the Game Summaries
   a. In how many games is a team winning after two periods of play? _____
   b. In how many of these games did that same team win the game?___
   c. Divide b by a to calculate the probability _____%

In the NHL what is the probability that a team winning at the end of three periods will win the game? _____%

Mostly Measurement
NHL Official Dimensions of Rink Surface

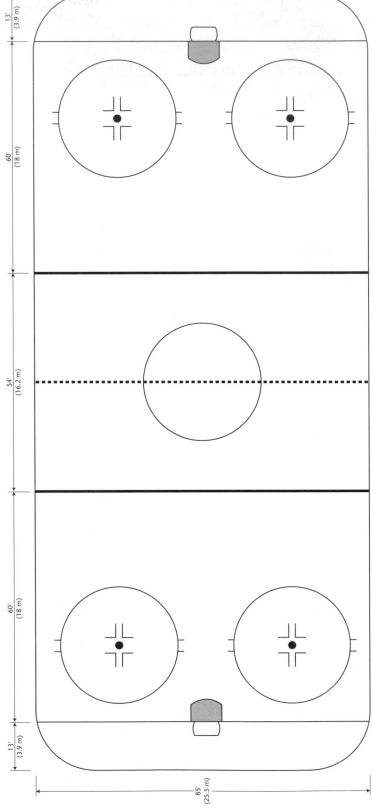

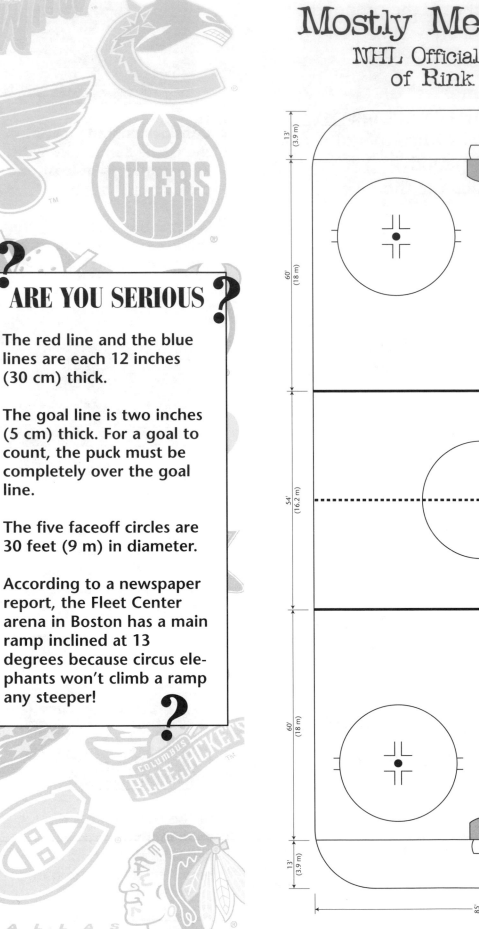

ARE YOU SERIOUS ?

The red line and the blue lines are each 12 inches (30 cm) thick.

The goal line is two inches (5 cm) thick. For a goal to count, the puck must be completely over the goal line.

The five faceoff circles are 30 feet (9 m) in diameter.

According to a newspaper report, the Fleet Center arena in Boston has a main ramp inclined at 13 degrees because circus elephants won't climb a ramp any steeper!

1. Using the diagram on the oposite page, what is the length of an NHL rink? _____

2. Is the rink surface exactly 17,000 square feet (530 square metres), more than 17,000 square feet (530 square metres), or less than 17,000 square feet (530 square metres)?

_____

What is the reason for your answer.

3. The distance between the goalposts is 6 feet (1.8 m). A puck is 1 inch (2.5 cm) thick and 3 inches (7.5 cm) in diameter.

How many pucks, lying flat on the ice, could be placed in a row along the goal line between the two goalposts? _____

4. The goalie tries to stop the puck from going between the goalposts into the net. Between the goalposts is 6 feet (1.8 m) and the goal area is 4 feet (1.2 m) high.

What is the area actually guarded by the goalie? _____

5. NHL Official Rules state that a goalie's catching glove should have a "maximum perimeter of 50 inches (125 cm). The perimeter of the glove is the distance around the glove."

Take a string of that length to help you design a goalie's catching glove. Compare your design with a friend's.

CALCULATOR CORNER

About 35 pucks are used during each NHL game. In the 1998/99 season 1107 regular season games were played.

If all the pucks used in the 1998/99 season were stacked up in one column, how tall would the column of pucks be (the size of a puck is given in question 3)? _____

The CN Tower in Toronto is the world's tallest free-standing structure at about 1843 feet (553 m). Which is taller, the column of pucks or the CN Tower? _____

An official NHL puck must weigh between 5 1/2 (156 g) and 6 ounces (170 g). What weighs more, a 10 pound (4.55 kg) bag of potatoes or the pucks used in an NHL game? _____

How many pucks do you weigh? _____

The Puck Stops Here

The goalie's job is to prevent the other team from scoring goals. How well the goalie does this is sometimes measured by his Goals-Against Average or GAA. The smaller the GAA the better the goalie.

In the first 13 seasons of his NHL career, Patrick Roy had a 2.69 GAA. This means that Roy allowed on average 2.69 goals per game or a little over two-and-one-half goals per game.

1. Rank Roy's season from 1 to 13, from smallest GAA to largest GAA.

	GAA	RANK
1985/86	3.35	
1986/87	2.93	
1987/88	2.90	
1988/89	2.47	
1989/90	2.53	
1990/91	2.71	
1991/92	2.36	
1992/93	3.20	
1993/94	2.50	
1994/95	2.97	
1995/96	2.78	
1996/97	2.32	
1997/98	2.39	

2. Let's compare these goalies' GAA during the regular season and in the playoffs through their careers.

Player	Regular Season	Playoffs
ED BELFOUR	2.57	2.35
MARTIN BRODEUR	2.16	1.84
DOMINIK HASEK	2.34	2.22
CHRIS OSGOOD	2.33	2.14
PATRICK ROY	2.69	2.38

Which player made the most improvement from the regular season to the playoffs? _____

Which goalie was most consistent in the regular season and playoffs?

_____

Another way to tell how well a goalie is doing is by his "Save Percent."

Chris Osgood's Save Percent or S% as he led Detroit to the Stanley Cup in 1997/98 was .918. This means that Osgood stopped 91.8% of the shots-on-goal.

3. In those same playoffs, four other goalies did even better. They were Ed Belfour (.922), Dominik Hasek (.938), Curtis Joseph (.928), and Olaf Kolzig (.941)

Which goalie had the best Save Percent?

_____

4. Very few goalies are traded during the season. Sean Burke was an exception. In 1997/98 Burke was traded from Carolina to Vancouver to Philadelphia.

Here are Burke's S% at each stop:

Carolina	.899
Vancouver	.876
Philadelphia	.913

Where did Burke have his best S%?_____

His worst? _____

Calculating Goalies

Using a calculator in this section may prove helpful.

To find a goalie's Goals-Against Average, multiply the number of goals allowed times 60, then divide this answer by the number of minutes played. The answer is expressed correct to two decimal places.

As a formula: **GAA = 60 x GA ÷ MIN**

For example, in his first full season in the NHL in 1990/91, Dominik Hasek was the first goalie in 20 years to have a GAA under 2.00. That season Hasek played 3358 minutes and allowed 109 goals.

> **GAA**
> **= 60 x 109 ÷ 3358**
> **= 1.947578...**

Therefore Hasek's GAA was 1.95.

1. Circle the goalie who had the NHL's best GAA in 1997/98.

	GA	MIN	GAA
Ed Belfour	112	3581	____
Martin Brodeur	130	4128	____

2. Consider these three seasons in Dominik Hasek's career.

HASEK	GA	MIN
1995/96	161	3417
1996/97	153	4037
1997/98	147	4220

a. Two of these seasons Hasek won the Hart Trophy as the NHL's Most Valuable Player (MVP). By examining the above chart decide which of the seasons he was NOT the MVP. _____

b. Calculate Hasek's GAA only for the season it was smallest! _____

Now let's examine Save Percent.

To calculate a goalie's Save Percent: from 1.000, subtract the number of goals-against divided by the number of shots-against. The answer is expressed as a decimal correct to three places.

As a formula: **S% = 1 – (GA ÷ SA)**

For example, midway through the 1998/99 season Mike Richter allowed 117 goals against and had 1231 shots against.

$$S\%$$
$$= 1 - 117 \div 1231$$
$$= .904955...$$

Therefore Richter's Save Percent was .905. This also happened to be the average Save Percent for all NHL goalies at that point in the season.

Discuss with a friend or family member whether the best way to compare goalies is with GAA or S%!

3. Among goalies who had played at least 50 games, these three goalies had the best Save Percent in the NHL in 1997/98. Rank them in order from 1 to 3 with 1 being the best.

	GA	SA	S%	RANK
Tom Barrasso	122	1556	____	____
Dominik Hasek	147	2149	____	____
Olaf Kolzig	139	1729	____	____

Power Play

Because of a penalty one team may have more players on the ice than the other team. The team with more players on the ice is said to be on a "power-play." The team with fewer players on the ice is said to be "short-handed."

A calculator will prove useful in solving these **power play** problems.

In the 1997/98 NHL season

1. Teams had 9884 power-play opportunities and scored 1491 times. What percent of these opportunities ended up in a power-play goal? _____

2. Dallas had the best power-play record with 77 goals in 385 opportunities. What was Dallas' power-play percent? _____

3. Tampa Bay had the weakest power-play with only 33 goals in 353 chances. What was Tampa Bay's power-play percent? _____

4. Even with fewer players on the ice, sometimes a team is able to score a short-handed goal. This happened 260 times in 1066 games. You would expect to see a short-handed goal about once every _____ games.

5. An exciting feature in NHL hockey is "the penalty shot." In this situation a player tries to score on a goalie without other players involved. It is just one-on-one! In 1997/98 there were 34 penalty shots. Sixteen were successful.

Is this more than or less than half the time?

_____

In a Game Summary on February 15, 1999 there was a section which read:

> Power Plays (goals-chances) —
> Chicago:1-4; Ottawa:1-6

This means that Chicago scored once on 4 power-play opportunities — a 1/4 or 25% success rate.

Ottawa scored once with 6 opportunities — 1/6 or 17% success rate.

In this game we would say that Chicago had the better power play.

6. Using the Game Summaries on pages 58-64, in how many games did
   a. Neither team score a power-play goal? ____
   b. Only one team score on the power play? ____
   c. Both teams score on the power play? ____

   Total   40

CALCULATOR CORNER

How important is the power play in determining who wins the game?

In the Game Summaries on pages 58-64, circle the games where the teams had a different power-play success rate.
How many such games are there?_____

In these games, circle the team with the better power-play.

In how many of these games did the team with the better power play:
win? ____   tie? ____
lose? ____

In what percent of these games did the team with the better power play win? ____

Overtime

During the regular NHL season, if the game is tied at the end of the third period, then the teams play five minutes of "sudden-death" overtime. As soon as one team scores the game is over, one team winning the other losing! If no team scores in the five minutes then the game is a tie.

Calculators will be helpful for these questions.

1. In 1997/98 in the NHL regular season 1066 games were played and 219 went into overtime.

What percent of games went into overtime? _____

2a. In 54 of these 219 games a goal was scored in overtime. Half the time the home team won.

What percent of games that went into overtime resulted in the tie being broken? _____

b. In the 40 Game Summaries from 1998/99 on pages 58-64, we have nine games going into overtime.

In how many of the these overtime games would you expect an overtime goal, assuming results were the same as in 1997/98? _____

Check the Game Summaries to see if you are right!

In the NHL playoffs, sudden-death overtime continues until one team scores. There is no five-minute limit!

One of the longest games was in the 1996 playoffs when Petr Nedved scored the winner at 79:15 of overtime. It took 79 minutes and 15 seconds of overtime to break the tie.

In the 1998 playoffs, the players in the chart won games in overtime with a goal. The amount of overtime played is also given.

3. Who scored the fastest goal? ____

4. Who scored the slowest goal? ____

5. Place the times in order from fastest to slowest. From this new list what was the middle time? (The time where half the times were more and half the times were less.) _____

   In mathematics this "middle" number is known as the "median," and is often used to describe "average."

6. Round each time to the nearest minute. Find the "average" time by adding the rounded times and dividing the total by the number of games.

   _____

   This type of "average" is called the "mean" by mathematicians.

7. A third way to describe average is the "mode" — the number or numbers that occurs most frequently in a list.

   Using the list of rounded times what is the mode? _____

   In this situation does it make sense to consider average as median, mean, or mode? Talk to a friend about this.

PLAYER	TIME	Rounded TIME
Bruce Gardiner	5:58	
Benoit Brunet	18:43	
Darren Van Impe	20:54	
Alexei Yashin	2:47	
Joe Juneau	26:31	
Joe Sakic	15:25	
Andrei Zyuzin	6:31	
Michal Grosek	5:40	
Mike Keane	3:43	
Brian Bellows	15:24	
Geoff Sanderson	2:37	
Benoit Hogue	13:07	
Michael Peca	21:24	
Brendan Shanahan	31:12	
Todd Krygier	3:01	
Peter Bondra	9:37	
Jamie Langenbrunner	0:46	
Joe Juneau	6:24	
Kris Draper	15:24	

PLAYER	TIME	Rounded TIME

THE STANLEY CUP
Predicting The Winner

At the end of the NHL playoffs two teams remain. These two teams then play in the Stanley Cup Final — the winner receiving the prized Stanley Cup! Each member of the winning team has his name engraved on the Stanley Cup.

Look on the cover of this book and you'll see how important the Stanley Cup victory in 1998 was to Detroit captain, Steve Yzerman.

As the playoffs begin millions of fans try to predict who will win the Stanley Cup. Some look to the regular season for clues.

Q Does the team with the best record during the regular season usually win the Stanley Cup?

A No! From 1989 through 1998 the team with the best regular season record has won only 2 out of 10 years.

Q Does the team which has scored the most goals during the regular season usually win?

A No! This has happened only once in the same 10 years.

Q Does the best defensive team during the regular season usually win the Stanley Cup?

A No again! From 1989 through 1998, the team which allowed the fewest goals during the regular season never won the Stanley Cup!

OVERTIME

00:00

Use the chart on the opposite page. The teams split the first two games of the series. Find a pattern for predicting who will win the series.

Let's look at the results of the Stanley Cup Final Series below and see if we can find some patterns for picking the winner! The teams play a 4 out of 7 series. This means that the first team to win 4 games wins the series.

Season	Winner	Runner-up	Home Team Game 1	Game-by-Game Results						
				1	2	3	4	5	6	7
1997/98	D	W	D	D	D	D	D			
1996/97	D	Ph	Ph	D	D	D	D			
1995/96	Co	F	Co	Co	Co	Co	Co			
1994/95	J	D	D	J	J	J	J			
1993/94	R	V	R	V	R	R	R	V	R	
1992/93	M	LA	M	LA	M	M	M	M		
1991/92	P	Ch	P	P	P	P	P			
1990/91	P	S	P	S	P	S	P	P	P	
1989/90	E	B	B	E	E	B	E	E		
1988/89	Ca	M	Ca	Ca	M	M	Ca	Ca	Ca	

Use the chart above to help you answer these questions.

1. In how many seasons did the team playing at home in Game 1 win the Stanley Cup?

_____

2. In how many seasons was the Stanley Cup won by the team which won
   a.   The first game of the series? _____
   b.   The second game of the series? ____
   c.   The third game of the series? _____

3a.   How many times did one team win the first two games of the series? _____
   b.   How many times did that team win the Stanley Cup? _____

Code:

B	Boston
Ca	Calgary
Ch	Chicago
Co	Colorado
D	Detroit
E	Edmonton
F	Florida
J	New Jersey
LA	Los Angeles
M	Montreal
P	Pittsburgh
Ph	Philadelphia
R	New York Rangers
S	Minnesota North Stars*
V	Vancouver
W	Washington

*Transferred to Dallas, 1993/94

Reading An NHL Game Summary

Colorado 7
at Florida   5

First Period

1. Fla, Kvasha 11 (Mellanby, Parrish) 11:42 (pp)
2. Fla, Bure 11 (Hedican) 14:36 (sh)

Penalties-Col bench 9:48, Svehla Fla 14:20

Second Period

3. Fla, Bure 12 (Whitney, Svehla) 4:41 (pp)
4. Fla, Bure 13 (Kozlov, Niedermayer) 10:47 (pp)
5. Fla, Mellanby 15 (Dvorak, Hedicon) 15:12
6. Col, Forsberg 19 (Sakic) 18:11

Penalties-Bure Fla 1:22, Drury Col 2:46, Laus Fla, Odgers Col 5:17, Dvorak Fla 5:28, Sakic Col 9:08, Foote Col 9:45, Butsayev Fla 19:00

Third Period

7. Col, Lemieux 22 (Deadmarsh, Forsberg) 0:17 (pp)
8. Col, Forsberg 20 (Drury, Ozolinsh) 7:15
9. Col, Deadmarsh 19 (Forsberg, Sakic) 15:00 (pp)
10. Col, Drury 14 (Podein, Donovan) 15:41
11. Col, Hejduk 9 (Sakic, Forsberg) 17:40
12. Col, Forsberg 21, 18:29

Penalties-Yelle Col 3:57, Niedermayer Fla 13:17

Shots

Colorado	9	7	18 - 34
Florida	11	9	8 - 28

Power plays (goals-chances)
Col 2-5; Florida 3-5

Do you understand the Game Summary
on the opposite page?

After studying the Game Summary, try this test.

1. Who scored the first goal of the game?

_____

2. On which Forsberg goal was only 1 assist
   awarded? _____

3. How many goals did Bure have this game?

_____

4. How many points (goals + assists) did
   Forsberg have? _____

5. In which period did Colorado have more
   shots-on-goal than Florida? _____

6. In this game which team had the more
   successful power play?

_____

7. What was the time difference between the
   11th and 12th goals of the game? _____

8. Which two players received a penalty
   at the same time? _____

_____

9. How many points did Joe Sakic have?

_____

10. How many goals had Forsberg scored in the
    season at the end of this game?_____

Give yourself a mark for each correct answer.
The test is out of 10! If you got 9 or 10, you're
an NHL All-Star!

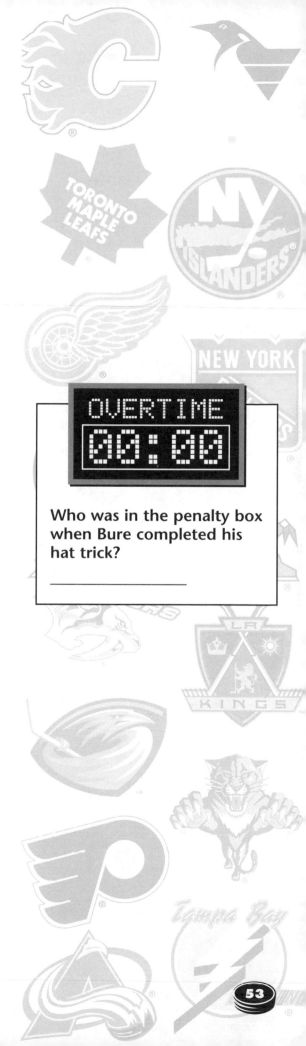

OVERTIME
00:00

Who was in the penalty box
when Bure completed his
hat trick?

_____

Breakaway Activities

Here are a few Challenges for you to really test your math stickhandling. For background information on Activity 1, see **The GAP** (page 18); Activity 2, see **Goals + Assists = Points** (page 16); Activity 3, see **Close Games** (page 24).

Activity 1
The Talent Scout

The purpose of this activity is to select five players who will do the best over the next week. You and a friend should each choose five different players and write their names below:

Your Team

Players	G	A	P
1 _____	____	____	____
2 _____	____	____	____
3 _____	____	____	____
4 _____	____	____	____
5 _____	____	____	____

Your Friend's Team

Players	G	A	P
1 _____	____	____	____
2 _____	____	____	____
3 _____	____	____	____
4 _____	____	____	____
5 _____	____	____	____

Over the next week record the number of goals, assists, and points made by each of your players. To find this information learn how to read a Game Summary on pages 52-53.

The top talent scout is the person whose players had the most points!

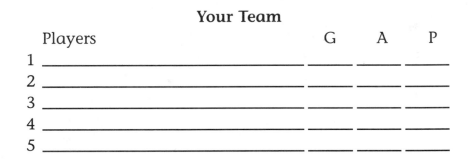

Activity 2
You Be the Coach (a card game)

Look for the NHL Scoring Leaders in the paper.

On a separate file card for each player, copy the first 10 players' names along with their goals and assists, but not their points.

After shuffling the cards, deal five cards face down to a friend and five to yourself.

Each person then turns over one card and calculates the points mentally on each card by adding goals plus assists.

The person with more points wins those two cards.

Each person now turns over a second card and play proceeds as before.

After all five cards have been played, the winner of the card game is the person with the most cards!

Activity 3
Creating a 3-D Graph

Record the scores for several days using a checkerboard and checkers. The illustration shows three 6-2 victories by the home team.

Find the scores in the newspaper.

From your checkerboard of collected scores:

What is the most popular score? _____

Does the home team usually win? ___

What scores won't fit on your checkerboard? _____

Are you surprised that certain scores haven't happened?

   Which ones? _____

Don't give up. Continue to look for them!

Answers

THE NHL TEAMS (pages 4-5)
Boston Bruins, Buffalo Sabres, Montreal Canadiens, Ottawa Senators, Toronto Maple Leafs; New Jersey Devils, New York Islanders, Philadelphia Flyers, New York Rangers, Pittsburgh Penguins; Carolina Hurricanes, Florida Panthers, Tampa Bay Lightning, Washington Capitals, Atlanta Thrashers; Chicago Black Hawks, Detroit Red Wings, Nashville Predators, Columbus Blue Jackets, St. Louis Blues; Calgary Flames, Colorado Avalanche, Edmonton Oilers, Minnesota Wild, Vancouver Canucks; Anaheim Mighty Ducks, Dallas Stars, Los Angeles Kings, Phoenix Coyotes, San Jose Sharks

AROUND THE WORLD (pages 6-7)
1. Canada 66, United States 18, Sweden 5, Czech Republic 6, Russia 12, Finland 1, Germany 1, Latvia 1, Poland 1; Philadelphia 22, Detroit 23, Colorado 23, New Jersey 23, Dallas 20; Total 111
2. 59%   3. 16%   4. 24%

YOU CAN'T TELL THE PLAYERS WITH-OUT A PROGRAM (pages 8-9)
1. Bondra   2. Roy   3. Fleury   4. Lidstrom
5. Bourque   6. Fleury   7. Yashin
8. Hasek   9. Belfour   10. Roenick + McInnes, Fedorov + Selanne, Lindros + Messier, Bourque + Hamrlik, Primeau + Pronger

HAPPY BIRTHDAY (pages 10-11)
1. May   2. 63, 27   3. 28   4. Jagr
5. Kariya 25   6. Hull 35

BIRTHDAY MATCHES (pages 12-13)
50 people: 97%, 40 people: 88%,
30 people: 70%, 20 people: 35%,
10 people: 10%

SCORE SEARCH (pages 14-15)
1. 5   2. Oct 11   3. Nov 12, Toronto 10, Chicago 3   4. Dec 14, St. Louis 0, Colorado 0   5. Oct 14   6. Nov 23, Dec 16
7. Nov 23, Dec 10   8. Oct 11, Oct 14, Dec 16

GOALS + ASSISTS = POINTS (pages 16-17)
1. Points: 83, 90, 91, 87, 90, 102, 87, 87, 86, 79   2a. Jagr   b. Forsberg   3a. Sakic   b. Lemieux   c. Kariya

THE GAP (pages 18-19)
1. 55 assists   2. Lindros 75, LeClair 35, Kariya 23   3. 33 goals
Cal Cor: 48-game season. Due to a lockout of the players, the season was shortened.

GREAT GOAL SCORERS (pages 20-21)
1. Hull 86, Lemieux 85   2. Hull   3. 82 goals   4. 51 goals   5. 40 goals
Cal Cor: every 16 games with a schedule of 26 x 82 ÷ 2 games

POINT PUZZLERS (pages 22-23)
1a. '80 1.734, '81 2.050, '82 2.650, '83 2.450, '84 2.770, '85 2.600, '86 2.688, '87 2.316;   b. 1985/86
c. 1983/84   2. Leach, fewer games same goals   3a. 1983 was better — more points in fewer games   b. 1988 was better — more points same games   4. Lindros: more points fewer games, Sakic: more points same number of games, Fedorov: same points fewer games, Leetch 10 more points in only one more game

CLOSE GAMES (pages 24-25)
1. 4,1,2,2,2,0,3,3,3,3,1,1,2,4,3,2,3,0,1,0,1,3,2
2. Winning margin:
0 goals, 3 games; 1 goal, 5 games; 2 goals, 6 games; 3 goals, 7 games; 4 goals, 2 games   3. 3 goals   Cal Cor: 1 goal 22%, 2 goals 26%, 3 goals 30%, 4 or more goals 9%.

HOME TEAM (pages 26-27)
1a. #1 V, #2 V, #3 V, #4 T, #5 T, #6 T, #7 H, #8 V, #9 V, #10 H, #11 T, #12 H, #13 H, #14 V, #15 H, #16 H, #17 H, #18 H, #19 H, #20 H, #21 V, #22 V, #23 V, #24 V, #25 V, #26 V, #27 V, #28 H, #29 T, #30 T, #31 H, #32 H, #33 H, #34 H, #35 V, #36 T, #37 H, #38 H, #39 H, #40 H   b. 19, 14, 7   c. Not really. The home team only won 19/40 games

NHL TEAM STANDINGS (pages 28-29)
1. 43 **2.** 16 **3.** 6 **4.** Toronto **5.** Dallas 43, Phoenix 42, Anaheim 17, San Jose 18, Los Angeles 4 **6a.** 22 games **b.** 30 games **c.** 84 games

A WINNING FORMULA (pages 30-31)
1. 61, 92, 89, 75, 77, 104, 70, 86, 77, 103, 84, 74, 75 - Teams with 77 or more points made the playoffs **2.** Colorado **3a.** 4 **b.** 22 **c.** 55 **d.** 53 **e.** 31, 66 **f.** 56 **g.** 15

THEY SHOOT, THEY SCORE (pages 32-33)
1a. 31,32,63 **b.** 24,28,52 **c.** 20,25,45 **d.** 38,36,74 **e.** 17,31,48 **f.** 22,37, 59 **g.** 25,37,62 Yes — The average is about 57 shots and there are 60 minutes in a hockey game. From the Game Summaries the average is about 56 shots-on-goal per game. **2.** 3 or 4 shots-on-goal per game **3a.** 33 games **b.** 17 games **c.** No. The winning team had more shots-on-goal only 17/33 times or only about half the time.

THE FIRST GOAL OF A GAME (pages 34-35)
1. A, B, C, D, F **2.** Win 24, Lose 9, Tie 7 **Cal Cor** 19 games, 13 games, 68%, 84%

UPDATING THE NHL TEAM STANDINGS (pages 36-37)
1. 164 **2.** 147 **3.** Dallas **4.** Which team scored the most goals? How many? **5.** Colorado 56,29,21,6,64,153,138
Edmonton 57,22,27,8,52,155,151
Calgary 57,20,28,9,49,145,166
Vancouver 58,18,33,7,43,143,190
OT: Bulldogs 4, Seals 1; Bulldogs 4, Tigers 1; Bulldogs 4, Falcons 1; Falcons 0, Tigers 0; Seals 5, Falcons 0; Seals 2, Tigers 2

WHAT'S THE PROBABILITY? (pages 38-39)
1a. 40 **b.** 33 **c.** 83% **2a.** 22 **b.** 18 **c.** 40 **d.** 55% **3a.** 28 **b.** 23 **c.** 79% **OT** 4/7=57%, 2/22 = 9%, 100%

MOSTLY MEASUREMENT (pages 40-41)
1. 200 feet (60m) **2.** A little less than 17,000 square feet (1530 square metres) because of the rounding in the corners **3.** 24 pucks **4.** 24 square feet (2.16 square metres) **Cal Cor** About 38,745 pucks were stacked. Each puck is 1 inch (2.5 cm). The stack would be almost 3229 feet (969m) high. The pucks are much taller than the CN Tower. If we choose 5.5 ounces (156 g), then the 35 pucks would weigh 192.5 ounces or a little over 12 pounds (5.474 kg). Bottom line is that the pucks weigh more than the bag of potatoes.

THE PUCK STOPS HERE (pages 42-43)
1. Top to bottom: #13, #10, #9, #4, #6, #7, #2, #12, #5, #11, #8, #1, #3 **2.** Brodeur improved 0.32 goals-per-game; Hasek was most consistent with a change of only 0.12 **3.** Kolzig **4.** Philadelphia, best; Vancouver, worst

CALCULATING GOALIES (pages 44-45)
1. Belfour 1.88, Brodeur 1.89 — Belfour was better. **2a.** 1995/96 — not MVP **b.** 1997/98 fewer goals allowed in more minutes — 2.09 **3.** Barrasso .922 #2, Hasek .932 #1, Kolzig .920 #3

POWER PLAY (pages 46-47)
1. 15% **2.** 20% **3.** 9% **4.** 4 games **5.** less than half **6a.** 10 **b.** 20 **c.** 10 **Cal Cor:** 28 games with different power play success rates; better power play— win 21, tie 4, lose 3; 75%, 89%

OVERTIME (pages 48-49)
1. 21% **2a.** 25% **b.** A reasonable guess would be 2; in fact, 2 games — #3 and — #23 provided an overtime goal. **3.** Langenbrunner **4.** Shanahan **5.** 9:37 **6.** 12 minutes **7.** the mode is 3,6,15

THE STANLEY CUP-PREDICTING THE WINNER (pages 50-51)
1. 7 **2a.** 7 **b.** 9 **c.** 7 **3a.** 6 **b.** 6 **OT:** the winner of the 4th game

READING AN NHL GAME SUMMARY (pages 52-53)
1. Kvasha **2.** The sixth goal of the game — Forsberg's first of the game. **3.** 3 **4.** 6 **5.** 3rd **6.** Florida **7.** 49 seconds **8.** Laus and Odgers **9.** 3 **10.** 21 **OT** Sakic and Foote

Game Summaries

1
Nashville   **2**
at Dallas   **1**

First Period
No scoring
Penalties—Fitzgerald Nash 7:27; Berehowsky Nash, Hull Dal 17:15; Modano Dal 19:35

Second Period
1. Dallas, Hull 26 (Modano, Lehtinen) 10:51
2. Nashville, Brunette 9 (Krivokrasov, Ronning) 16:14 (pp)
Penalties—Bouchard Nash, Verbeek Dal (double minor) 11:39; Hatcher Dal 15:20; Boughner Nash 18:19

Third Period
3. Nashville, Krivokrasov 19 (Bordeleau) 19:31
Penalties—None

Shots
Nashville	5	12	8	—25
Dallas	4	7	7	—18

Powerplay—Nashville: 1-3; Dallas: 0-2

2
Philadelphia   **4**
at Phoenix   **1**

First Period
1. Philadelphia, LeClair 36 (Lindros, Therien) 9:40
Penalty—Therien Pha 14:54

Second Period
2. Philadelphia, LeClair 37 (Jones) 10:19
3. Philadelphia, Tertyshny 1 (LeClair, Jones) 11:15
Penalties—Doan Phx 2:15; Tertyshny Pha 7:08; Forbes Pha 19:29

Third Period
4. Philadelphia, Desjardins 12 (LeClair, Jones) 3:39
5. Phoenix, Hansen 2 (Briere, Doig) 8:43
Penalties—None

Shots
Philadelphia	14	20	7	—41
Phoenix	14	10	9	—33

Power Play—Philadelphia: 0-1; Phoenix: 0-3

3
Los Angeles   **3**
at Detroit   **2**

First Period
1. Detroit, Shanahan 22 (Yzerman, Lidstrom), 14:15
Penalties—Holmstrom Det 6:31; Murray LA 8:16; Audette LA 10:57

Second Period
2. Detroit, Fedorov 17 (Brown, Holmstrom), 2:31
Penalties—McCarty Det, O'Donnell LA (major) 18:58

Third Period
3. Los Angeles, Audette 11 (Laperriere) 7:06
4. Los Angeles, Blake 5 (Pronger, Stumpel), 7:35
Penalties—None

Overtime
5. Los Angeles, Robitaille 31 (Audette, Stumpel), 1:57 (pp)
Penalty—Larionov Det 1:02

Shots
Los Angeles	15	8	14	3	—40
Detroit	11	7	7	1	—26

Power Play—Los Angeles 1-2; Detroit 0-2

4
Los Angeles   **2**
at Calgary   **2**

First Period
1. LA, Audette 10 (Blake, Jokinen) 13:11
Penalties—Dubinsky Cal 4:32; Stillman Cal, Jokinen LA 16:37

Second Period
2. Los Angeles, Jokinen 7 (Storr) 11:14 (pp)
3. Calgary, Housley 5 (Fleury, Morris) 15:47
Penalties—Shantz Cal 1:26; Robitaille LA (closing hand on puck) 6:49; Gauthier Cal 9:21; Murray LA, Smith Cal (unsportsmanlike conduct) 13:48

Third Period
4. Calgary, Fleury 29 (Morris) 9:48
Penalties—Housley Cal 12:06; Stumpel LA 17:14

Overtime
No scoring
Penalties—O'Donnell LA (minor major), Laperriere LA, Iginla Cal (minor, major, Wiemer 4:09

Shots
Los Angeles	12	9	11	1	—33
Calgary	8	9	6	4	—27

Power Play—Los Angeles: 1-5; Calgary: 0-3

5
Tampa Bay   **3**
at NY Islanders   **3**

First Period
1. Tampa Bay, Tucker 15 (Betik) 2:04
2. NY Islanders, Czerkawski 13 (Linden, Jonsson) 15:54
Penalties—Lecavalier TB 4:50; Skopintsev TB 9:15; Brewer NYI 18:36

Second Period
3. NY Islanders, Palffy 10 (Lapointe) 1:18
Penalties—Gratton TB 7:04; Skopintsev TB, Sacco NYI 13:55; Kubina TB 14:07; Tucker TB (minor, misconduct, game misconduct) 15:48

Third Period
4. Tampa Bay, Nylander 3 (Lecavalier, Betik) 6:09
5. NY Islanders, Palffy 11 7:10
6. TB, Lecavalier 9 (Kubina, Nylander) 10:29
Penalties—None

Overtime
No scoring
Penalties—None

Shots
Tampa Bay	7	11	7	0	—25
NY Islanders	6	9	9	5	—31

Power Play—Tampa Bay: 0-1; NY Islanders: 0-5

6
Chicago   **3**
at Nashville   **3**

First Period
1. Nash, Johnson 8 (Brunette, Yachmenev) 14:01
Penalties—Vopat Nash 2:39; Laflamme Chi 5:33; Janssens Chi, Lambert Nash (majors) 10:51

Second Period
2. Nash, Yachmenev 5 (Johnson) 0:41
3. Nash, Turcotte 4 (Fitzgerald, Boughner) 7:16
4. Chicago, Chelios 5 (Gilmour, Emerson) 8:20
5. Chicago, White 4 (Kilger, Emerson) 10:22

Penalties—Janssens Chi, Cote Nash (majors) 6:48; Gilmour Chi, Bouchard Nash (majors), Bouchard Nash 8.20, Zhamnov Chi 10:38; Muir Chi 12:06; Moreau Chi 15:42

Third Period
6. Chicago, Emerson 9 (Gilmour, Muir) 8:59

Penalties—Bouchard Nash 0:56; Amonte Chi, Vopat Nash 8:24; Amonte Chi, Gilmour Chi, Manson Chi, Fitzgerald Nash, Lambert Nash, Turcotte Nash, 20:00

Overtime
No scoring
Penalties—None

Shots
Chicago	8	12	10	4	—34
Nashville	7	12	6	2	—27

Power Play—Chicago: 0-3; Nashville: 0-4

7
New Jersey	**1**
at Detroit	**3**

First Period
1. Detroit, Yzerman 23, 15:36

Penalties—Brylin NJ 4:07; Oliwa NJ, McCarty Det (unsportsmanlike conduct) 7:06; Oliwa NJ, McCarty Det (major) 9:12; Draper Det 13:30; Kozlov Det 19:32

Second Period
2. Detroit, Larionov 10 (Kozlov, Ward) 6:31
3. New Jersey, Holik 23 (Brylin) 6:52
4. Detroit, Yzerman 24 (Osgood) 8:22 (pp)

Penalties—Arnott NJ 1:12; Holik NJ 7:02; Souray NJ 13:45

Third Period
No scoring
Penalty—Draper Det 15:36

Shots
New Jersey	6	4	12	—22
Detroit	11	8	8	—27

Power Play—New Jersey: 0-3; Detroit: 1-4

8
Anaheim	**5**
at Vancouver	**1**

First Period
1. Ana, Green 10 (Sandstrom, Rucchin), 18:32

Penalties—None

Second Period
2. Ana, Selanne 30 (Olausson, Rucchin), 2:40 (pp)
3. Ana, Selanne 31 (Sandstrom, McInnis), 7:03 (pp)
4. Ana, Kariya 25 (penalty shot), 19:19 (sh)

Penalties—Huscroft Van 1:55; Trnka Ana 4:44; Gagner Van 5:54; York Van 10:45; Anaheim (bench, delay of game) 16:29; Salei Ana 17:40; Ohlund Van 17:40; Cullen Ana 18:01; Trepanier Ana 18:47; Bertuzzi Van 18:47

Third Period
5. Van, Aucoin 14 (Gagner, Bertuzzi), 3:00 (pp)
6. Ana, McInnis 17 (Oluasson, Kariya) 5:48 (pp)

Penalties—Haller Ana 2:27; Kariya Ana 3:00; Muckalt Van 3:00; Scatchard Van 4:35; Green Ana 15:42; Marshall Ana 18:36

Shots
Anaheim	10	11	2	—23
Vancouver	7	5	14	—26

Power Play—Anaheim: 3-4; Vancouver: 1-6

9
Montreal	**3**
at Philadelphia	**1**

First Period
No scoring

Penalties—Tertyshny Phi :58; Damphousse Mon 8:36; Montreal bench, served by Savage 8:59

Second Period
1. Montreal, Recchi 11 (Corson, Weinrich), 4:46
2. Philadelphia, Lindros 33 (LeClair), 8:18
Penalties—None

Third Period
3. Montreal, Zholtok 5 (Malakhov, Recchi), 1:18 (pp)
4. Montreal, Koivu 11 (Brunet), 13:24 (sh)

Penalties—Lindros Phi :33; Zelepukin Phi 6:58; Weinrich Mon 12:06

Shots
Montreal	7	8	6	—21
Philadelphia	3	10	9	—22

Power Play—Montreal: 1-3; Philadelphia: 0-3

10
St. Louis	**1**
at Pittsburgh	**2**

First Period
1. Pittsburgh, Titov 5 (Straka, Jagr) 10:07
Penalties—Prong StL 3:30; Kesa Pgh 11:14; Galanov Pgh 14:21; Werenka Pgh 15:47

Second Period
2. St. Louis, Conroy 3 (Campbell, Demitra) 15:37
3. Pittsburgh, Lang 17 (Werenka) 18:42
Penalties—Yake StL 6:59; Persson StL 10:27; Barnes Pgh 13:23

Third Period
No scoring
Penalty—Pronger StL 19:45

Shots
St. Louis	7	15	8	—30
Pittsburgh	3	7	4	—14

Power Play—St. Louis: 0-4; Pittsburgh: 0-4

11
Carolina	**2**
at Toronto	**2**

First Period
1. Carolina, Primeau 26 (Sheppard) 13:54
Penalty—Battaglia Car 11:31

Second Period
2. Carolina, Kapanen 17 (Primeau, Sheppard) 12:53 (pp)
3. Toronto, Sundin 21 (Karpovtsev. Thomas) 14:48
Penalties—Karpovtsev Tor 11:22; Yushkevich Tor 16:38

Third Period
4. Toronto. McCauley 8 (McAllister, Johnson) 14:55

Penalties—Warriner Tor 2:41; Wesley Car 4:34; Coffey Car, Gelinas Car (misconduct) 11:58; Malik Car 15:37

Overtime
No scoring
Penalties—None

Shots
Carolina	13	13	4	1	—31
Toronto	12	8	10	1	—31

Power Play—Carolina: 1-3; Toronto: 0-4

12
Philadelphia	**3**
at Florida	**5**

First Period
No scoring

Penalties—Svehla Fla :15; Lindsay Fla 4:14; Jones Pha 8:36; Boyle Fla 9:28; Worrell Fla, Richardson Pha 11:54

Second Period
1. Philadelphia, Bureau 4 (Zubrus) 4:19
2. Philadelphia, Lindros 35 (LeClair, Jones) 5:01
3. Florida, Boyle 1 (Hicks, Worrell) 6:12
4. Florida, Mellanby 13 (Spacek, Muller) 6:57
5. Florida, Kvasha 10 (Boyle, Burke) 10:37 (pp)

Penalties—Desjardins Pha 9:02, Hull Pha 11:35; Kozlov Fla 12:06; Kozlov Fla 16:17

Third Period

6. Philadelphia, Desjardins 13 (Brind'Amour, Babych) 5:28 (pp)

7. Florida, Parrish 16 (Kvasha, Mellanby) 11:32 (pp)

8. Florida, Kozlov 11. 19:14 (en)

Penalties—Mellanby Fla 4:34; Therien Pha 7:59; Lindros Pha 10:36; Niedermayer Fla 16:03; Hicks Fla, Langkow Pha (majors) 18:32; Jones Fla, Mellanby Fla (minor, misconduct), Worrell Fla (misconduct) 19:43

Shots

Philadelphia	10	7	10	—27
Florida	8	10	6	—24

Power Play—Philadelphia: 1-7; Florida: 2-5

13

NY Islanders	1
at Carolina	4

First Period

1. Carolina, Primeau 25 (Wesley) 8:07

2. Carolina, O'Neill 12 (Kapanen, Kron) 17:10 (pp)

3. Carolina, Sheppard 20 (Battaglia) 17:46

Penalty—Lachance NYI 15:51

Second Period

No scoring

Penalties—Gelinas Car 6:03; Roberts Car 18:28

Third Period

4. NY Islanders, Nemchinov 7 (Lawrence) 2:19

5. Carolina, Sheppard 21 (Francis) 19:51 (en)

Penalties—Lachance NYI 5:32; Palffy NYI 8:24; Shappard Car 11:49

Shots

NY Islanders	7	8	14	—29
Carolina	15	14	8	—37

Power Play—NY Islanders: 0-3; Carolina: 1-3

14

Anaheim	2
at Edmonton	1

First Period

No scoring

Penalties—Salei Ana 8:13; Green Ana 17:05

Second Period

No scoring

Penalties—Grimson Ana (major) 3:22; Laraque Edm (major) 3:22; Lindgren Edm 3:28; Selanne Ana 7:55; Marchant Edm 15:27

Third Period

1. Anaheim, Selanne 32 (Kariya) 11:12

2. Edmonton, Murray 12 (Falloon, Smyth) 12:56

3. Anaheim, Kariya 26 (Rucchin) 14:56

Penalties—Green Ana 3:46; Selivanov Edm 4:11; Haller Ana 5:41

Shots

Anaheim	5	9	10	—24
Edmonton	16	10	7	—33

Power Play—Anaheim: 0-2; Edmonton: 0-5

15

Vancouver	0
at Chicago	4

First Period

1. Chicago, Gilmour 14 (Daze, Amonte) 2:32 (pp)

2. Chicago, Kilger 11 4:37

Penalties—Hendrickson Van 1:37; Brown Chi 6:38; Gilmour Chi 18:16

Second Period

3. Chicago, Kilger 12 (Olczyk) 13:26

4. Chicago, Amonte 29 (Leroux, Gilmour) 18:10

Penalties—Brashear Van (major) 3:04; Probert Chi (major) 3:04; Hendrickson Van 4:34; Hendrickson Van 11:29; Muir Chi 11:29; Brown Chi 18:31

Third Period

No scoring

Penalties—Strudwick Van 1:27; May Van (major) 17:20; Brown Chi (major) 17:20

Shots

Vancouver	6	10	13	—29
Chicago	3	8	3	—14

Power Play—Vancouver: 0-3; Chicago: 1-3

16

Tampa Bay	1
at Ottawa	5

First Period

No scoring

Penalties— Prospal Ott 2:00; Arvedson Ott 5:38; Larocque TB 9:37; Bannister TB 14:41

Second Period

1. Ottawa, McEachern 19 (Dackell, York) 8:04

2. Ottawa, Alfredsson 4 (Yashin, Redden) 12:30 (pp)

3. Ottawa, McEachern 20 (Yashin) 15:01

4. Tampa Bay, Sillinger 1 (Selivanov) 17:28

Penalties—Samuelsson TB 4:45; Larouque TB (holding the puck) 12:01; Clark TB 19:50; Bonk Ott 19:50

Third Period

5. Ottawa, Arvedson 9 (Bonk, York) 6:00

6. Ottawa, Yashin 16 (Dackell, Johansson) 8:50 (pp)

Penalties—McCarthy TB 7:09; Richer TB 10:39; Richer TB 14:53

Shots

Tampa Bay	3	9	8	—20
Ottawa	9	16	10	—35

Power Play—Tampa Bay: 0-2; Ottawa: 2-7

17

Florida	1
at Dallas	2

First Period

No scoring

Penalties—Kozlov Fla 1:28; Sydor Dal 2:18; Worrell Fla 11:05; Hicks Fla, Nieuwendyk Dal 12:45; Hicks Fla, Verbeek Dal (majors) 19:38

Second Period

No scoring

Penalties—Laus Fla 9:38; Wells Fla 15:24; Dvorak Fla 18:59

Third Period

1. Dallas, Langenbrunner 8 (Verbeek) 4:49

2. Dallas, Hatcher 8 (Nieuwendyk) 9:29 (pp)

3. Florida, Dvorak 9 (Spacek, Kozlov) 16:14

Penalties—Keane Dal 2:14; Murphy Fla 8:03

Shots

Florida	3	3	10	—16
Dallas	12	9	8	—29

Power Play—Florida: 0-2; Dallas: 1-6

18

Pittsburgh	1
at NY Islanders	3

First Period

No scoring

Penalties—Harlock NYI 16:24; Kovalev Pit 17:05

Second Period

1. New York, Reichel 17 (Palffy, Lapointe) 12:24

Penalties—Werenka Pgh 2:27; Pilon NYI 5:57; Kasparaitis Pgh 13:13; New York bench, served by Smolinski 14:45; Titov Pgh 15:21; Kasparaitis Pgh 16:32

Third Period

2. New York, Lawrence 7 (Nemchinov, Lapointe) 6:20

3. New York, Linden 14 (Czerkawksi, Jonsson) 9:00 (pp)

4. Pittsburgh, Miller 14 (Hrdina, Jagr) 17:54

Penalties—Lang Pgh (double minor) 6:48; Richter NYI 9:26

Shots

Pittsburgh	8	6	7	—21
NY Islanders	12	12	7	—31

Power Play—Pittsburgh: 0-4; NY Islanders: 1-6

19

NY Rangers	2
at Calgary	6

First Period
1. Calgary, Fleury 30 (Shantz, Smith) 2:47
2. Calgary, Bure 13 (Fleury, Housley) 5:09 (pp)

Penalties—Hulse Cal :27; Fedyk NYR 3:15; Gauthier Cal 6:38; Nedved NYR 13:26

Second Period
3. Calgary, Housley 6 (Landry) 10:07
4. NY Rangers, Stevens 15 (Gretzky, MacLean) 12:37 (pp)
5. Calgary, Stillman 16 12:50

Penalties—Simpson Cal 10:07; Smith Cal 10:40

Third Period
6. Calgary, Stillman 17 (Gauthier, Dubinsky) 5:00 (sh)
7. Calgary, Housley 7 (Iginla, Smith) 6:15
8. NY Rangers, Malhotra 6 15:39

Penalties—Hulse Cal 3:35; Wiemer Cal 8:45

Shots
NY Rangers	10	9	12	—31
Calgary	11	18	9	—38

Power Play—NY Rangers: 1-6; Calgary: 1-2

20

Phoenix	1
at Florida	7

First Period
1. Florida, Mellanby 12 (Whitney, Niedermayer) :33
2. Florida, Kozlov 10 (Dvorak, Carkner) 6:59
3. Florida, Dvorak 10 (Kozlov, Boyle) 18:30
4. Florida, Lindsay 9 (Kvasha, Warrener) 19:06

Penalties—Carkner Fla 3:27; Hansen Phx, Warrener Fla (major) 5:34; Cummins Phx, Laus Fla 8:53; Tkachuk Phx 11:08; Carkner Fla 13:48

Second Period
5. Florida, Lindsay 10 (Hicks, Warrener) 9:17
6. Phoenix, Tocchet 21 (Roenick, Tverdovsky) 17:57 (pp)

Penalties—Phoenix bench (too many men), served by Cummins 5:40; Worrell Fla 16:48

Third Period
7. Florida, Svehla 7 (Whitney, Burke) 1:45 (pp)
8. Florida, Spacek 3 (Kozlov) 3:19 (sh)

Penalties—Doan Phx :50; Worrell Fla 2:15; Tkachuk Phx, Worrell Fla 7:36; Cummins Phx 13:05

Shots
Phoenix	10	15	10	—35
Florida	12	9	9	—30

Power Play—Phoenix: 1-4; Florida: 1-4

21

Dallas	2
at San Jose	1

First Period
1. Dallas, Modano 14 (Hull, Lehtinen) :46

Penalties—Rouse SJ 2:28; Ludwig Dal 17:08; Lowry SJ 19:50

Second Period
2. Dallas, Zubov 6 (Hrkac, Marshall) 1:51

Penalties—Ricci SJ 3:58; Murphy SJ 8:13

Third Period
3. San Jose, Matteau 2 (Ricci, Rouse) 2:10

Penalties—Skrudland Dal 2:23; Marshall Dal 7:47

Shots
Dallas	5	9	6	—20
San Jose	8	8	16	—32

Power Play—Dallas: 0-4; San Jose: 0-3

22

Washington	3
at New Jersey	2

First Period
1. Washington, Bellows 7 (Nikolishin, Halverson) 19:01

Penalties—Bondra Was 8:26, Lakovic NJ 11:59

Second Period
2. Washington, Pivonka 3 (Bondra, Juneau) 7:18

Penalties—Elias NJ 5:15; New Jersey bench 13:40

Third Period
3. Washington, Juneau 7 (Klee, Johansson) :35
4. New Jersey, Sharifijanov 5 (Holik, Rolston) 3:34
5. New Jersey, Elias 7 (Morrison, Pandolfo) 19:12

Penalties—Bellows Was 11:10; Gonchar Was 16:42

Shots
Washington	9	12	4	—25
New Jersey	15	8	18	—41

Power Play—Washington: 0-3; New Jersey: 0-3

23

Toronto	3
at Buffalo	2

First Period
1. Toronto, Domi 5 (Thomas, Sundin) 4:14

Penalties—Brown Buf 4:20; Karpovtsev Tor 11:37; K.King Tor 19:06

Second Period
2. Toronto, Sullivan 12 (Sundin, Thomas) 2:21 (pp)
3. Buffalo, Ward 16 (Peca, Zhitnik) 3:54

Penalties—Peca Buf 1:19; Domi Tor, Ray Buf (majors) 2:53; Markhov Tor 7:57; Shannon Buf 14:24

Third Period
4. Buffalo, Satan 25 (Grosek, Wilson) 10:23

Penalty—Holzinger Buf 15:09

Overtime
5. Toronto, Sundin 19 (Thomas) 4:04

Penalty—Rasmussen Buf (misconduct) 3:26

Shots
Toronto	8	13	5	3	—29
Buffalo	10	9	5	3	—27

Power Play—Toronto: 1-4; Buffalo: 0-3

24

Boston	6
at Chicago	3

First Period
1. Boston, Bourque 5 (Thornton, Robitaille) 11:25 (pp)
2. Boston, Khristich 22 (Ellett) 12:29
3. Boston, Khristich 23 (Bourque, Samsonov) 19:36

Penalties—Emerson Chi 6:33; Laflamme Chi 10:23; Mann Bos, Simpson Chi 15:41; DiMaio Bos, Gilmour Chi 17:22

Second Period
4. Boston, Mann 1 (Carter) 1:40
5. Chicago, Zhamnov 11 (Emerson, Gilmour) 8:17
6. Chicago, Chelios 8 12:11 (sh)
7. Chicago, Daze 13 (Laflamme, White) 17:28 (pp)

Penalties—Gill Bos 4:04; Baumgartner Bos, Brown Chi (major) Amonte Chi 8:44; Leroux Chi 10:58; Ferraro Bos 15:35

Third Period
8. Boston, Samsonov 20 (Khristich, Allison) 5:35
9. Boston, Khristich 24 (Allison) 15:31

Penalties—Moreau Chi 9:04; DiMaio Bos, Zhamnov Chi 14:01; Baumgartner Bos 18:39

Shots
Boston	7	8	13	—28
Chicago	9	12	10	—31

Power Play—Boston: 1-5; Chicago: 1-3

25

Detroit   **4**
at NY Rangers   **2**

First Period

1. Detroit, Fedorov 15 (Yzerman, Shanahan) 1:12
2. Detroit, Yzerman 22 (Shanahan, Murphy) 6:31 (sh)
3. Detroit, Klima 1 (Larionov, Kozlov) 14:36

Penalties—Fedorov Det 3:48; MacLean NYR 4:27; Brown Det 5:52; Fedyk NYR 9:40; Harvey NYR 15:24

Second Period

4. NY Rangers, Savard 8 (Fedyk, Stevens) 12:40

Penalties—Harvey NYR 9:05; Murphy Det 19:33

Third Period

5. NY Rangers, Fedyk 3 (Schneider) 4:30
6. Detroit, Lidstrom 10 (Yzerman, Fedorov) 19:33 (en)

Penalties—Lacroix NYR 11:46; Fedorov Det 12:51; McCarty Det, Savard NYR 18:27; Tamer NYR, Stevens NYR 19:52

Shots

Detroit	13	8	9	—30
NY Rangers	11	10	10	—31

Power Play—Detroit: 0-7; NY Rangers: 0-4

26

Chicago   **3**
at St. Louis   **1**

First Period

1. Chicago, Gilmour 15 (Muir, Emerson) 6:34
2. Chicago, Gilmour 16 (Chelios) 9:34

Penalty—Brown Chi 13:19

Second Period

3. St. Louis, MacInnis 17 (Turgeon, Demitra) 7:38

Penalties—Laflamme Chi, Picard StL (double minor) 2:16; Turgeon StL 9:16; Conroy StL 10:11; Janssens Chi 13:27

Third Period

4. Chicago, Zhamnov 12 (Olczyk, Zmolek) 17:50

Penalty—Manson Chi 10:30

Shots

Chicago	7	5	4	—16
St. Louis	10	9	7	—26

Power Play—Chicago: 0-2; St. Louis 0-3

27

Montreal   **6**
at NY Rangers   **3**

First Period

1. Montreal, Rucinsky 14 (Brunet) 4:25
2. Montreal, Hoglund 7 (Zholtok) 4:43
3. Montreal, Carson 9 (Recchi, Koivu) 5:32

Penalties—Tamer NY 11:15; Corson Mon 17:36

Second Period

4. NY Rangers, Knuble 10 (Savard, Brennan) 6:32 (pp)
5. Montreal, Damphousse 11 (Quintal, Brunet) 8:40

Penalties—Corson Mon :16; Stevenson Mon (major: game misconduct) 2:42; Ulanov Mon (double minor) 13:14; Montreal bench, served by Zholtok 17:26; Leetch NY 17:56

Third Period

6. Montreal, Thornton 4 (Poulin, Brunet) 4:47
7. NY Rangers, Knuble 11 (Leetch, Schneider) 10:51 (pp)
8. NY Rangers, Nedved 11 (Knuble, Samuelsson) 13:00
9. Montreal, Quintal 6 (Koivu, Malakhov) 14:02

Penalties—Thornton Mon 9:16; Harvey NY 11:44; Rucinsky Mon 12:18

Shots

Montreal	21	12	13	—46
NY Rangers	13	15	10	—38

Power Play—Montreal: 0-2; NY Rangers: 2-8

28

Florida   **2**
at Carolina   **3**

First Period

1. Carolina, Primeau 20 (Francis, Sheppard) 10:42 (pp)
2. Florida, Whitney 14 (Mellanby, Murphy) 12:06

Penalties—Carkner Fla, Pratt Car :08; Laus Fla 9:54; O'Neill Car 13:46; Wesley Car, Gagner Fla 15:50; Burke Fla, served by Murphy, 19:46

Second Period

No scoring
Penalties—Malik Car 6:40; Kvasha Fla 11:56; Svehla Fla 16:55

Third Period

3. Carolina, Kapanen 12 (Francis, Roberts) 5:13
4. Florida, Ratchuk 1 (Kozlov, Svehla) 14:00
5. Carolina, Wesley 3 (Francis) 19:18

Penalties—Roberts Car 7:51; Pratt Car, Mellanby Fla (9:19; Garpenlov Fla 11:20

Shots

Florida	6	3	6	—15
Carolina	5	6	12	—23

Power Play—Florida: 0-3; Carolina: 1-5

29

Colorado   **1**
at Dallas   **1**

First Period

1. Dallas, Hull 25 (Sydor, Modano) 7:58 (pp)

Penalties—Corbet Col :44; Roy Col (slashing; served by Kaminsky) 7:19; Heiduk Col 9:46; Ludwig Dal 12:31; Ozolinsh Col 14:17

Second Period

2. Colorado, Drury 12 (Deadmarsh, Forsberg) 11:30

Penalties—Lehtinen Dal 6:10; Matvichuk Dal (double minor) Corbet Col 8:29; Klemm Col 12:29; Forsberg Col 18:15

Third Period

No scoring
Penalties—Carbonneau Dal, Lemieux Col 7:21; Modano Dal 8:11; Forsberg Col 11:21

Overtime

No scoring
Penalties—None

Shots

Colorado	8	6	4	0	—18
Dallas	8	6	8	2	—24

Power Play—Colorado: 0-4; Dallas: 1-7

30

Edmonton   **1**
at Los Angeles   **1**

First Period

1. Los Angeles, Blake 3 (Audette, Perreault) 5:31 (pp)

Penalty—Smyth Edm 4:26

Second Period

2. Edmonton, Smyth 3 (Guerin, Mironov) 7:19 (pp)

Penalties—Reirden Edm :52; Stumpel LA (double minor) 6:22; McAmmond Edm 8:34; Norstrom LA 17:31; McSorley Edm 20:00

Third Period

No scoring
Penalties—Guerin Edm (major) Audette LA (major, game misconduct) 8:08; Visheau LA 9:29; Marchant Edm 11:30; Visieau LA 17:28

Overtime

No scoring
Penalties—None

Shots

Edmonton	9	13	9	2	—33
Los Angeles	8	7	13	2	—30

Power Play—Edmonton: 1-5; Los Angeles: 1-5

31

San Jose   1
at Washington   3

First Period

No scoring

Penalties—Svelkovsky Was 5:45; Tinordi Was 9:43; Rouse SJ 12:20; Konowalchuk Was 14:01

Second Period

1. San Jose, Friesen 18 (Ricci) 11:57 (pp)
2. Washington, Gonchar 12 (Oates, Svelkovsky) 13:04 (pp)

Penalties—Heins SJ (closing hand on puck) 8:54; Gonchar Was 11:15; Craven SJ 12:48; Lowry SJ, Svelkovsky Was 13:14; Ciccone Was 17:37

Third Period

3. Washington, Gonchar 13 (Nikolishin, Konowalchuk) 11:14 (pp)
4. Washington, Black 3 (Reekie) 19:02 (en)

Penalties—Eagles Was 2:26; Konowalchuk Was, Nolan SJ 3:49; Matteau SJ 9:18; Klee Was 13:43; Eagles Was, Miller Was (minor, misconducts) 20:00

Shots

San Jose	6	5	4	—15
Washington	4	8	9	—21

Power Play—San Jose: 1-7; Washington: 2-4

32

Montreal   1
at Ottawa   3

First Period

1. Ottawa, Johansson 18 (Prospal) 6:11
2. Montreal, Brunet 13 (Quintal, Damphousse) 17:54

Penalties—Redden Ott :42; Quintal Mon 1:55; Laukkanen Ott 7:52; Redden Ott 18:21

Second Period

3. Ottawa, Johansson 19 (Alfredsson, Prospal) 14:32

Penalties—Thornton Mon 12:20

Third Period

4. Ottawa, Yashin 28 (Dackell, Redden) 7:43

Penalties—Berg Ott (interference) 3:39; Dackell Ott (obstruction-tripping) 10:26

Shots

Montreal	13	6	6	—25
Ottawa	8	8	12	—28

Power Play—Montreal: 0-5; Ottawa: 0-2

33

Ottawa   2
at Boston   5

First Period

1. Boston, Taylor 4 (Axelsson, Bourque) 1:31
2. Ottawa, McEachern 27 (Alfredsson, Kravchuk) 10:01
3. Boston, Allison 16 (Khristich, Carter) 12:29
4. Boston, Carter 9 (Allison, Khristich) 17:40

Penalties—None

Second Period

5. Boston, Mann 2 (Thornton, Robitaille) 12:01 (pp)

Penalties—York Ott 10:02; Belanger Bos 15:24; Prospal Ott (major) Laukkanen Ott (minor, misconduct), Axelsson Bos, DiMaio Bos (minor, misconduct), Gill Bos (major) 19:00

Third Period

6. Ottawa, Alfredsson 13 (Yashin, Van Allen) 1:45
7. Boston, Mann 3 (Baumgartner, Thornton) 12:03

Penalties—Bourque Bos 3:00; Martins Ott 3:17; Thornton Bos (intent to injure major-game misconduct) 16:56; Hossa Ott 18:22

Shots

Ottawa	6	9	13	—28
Boston	14	11	7	—32

Power Play—Ottawa: 0-4; Boston: 1-2

34

San Jose   2
at Buffalo   4

First Period

1. Buffalo, Sanderson 10 (Holzinger, Patrick) 2:01

Penalties—Matteau SJ (minor, major) Wilson Buf (instigator, major, misconduct) 4:12; Lowry SJ 5:52; Grand-Pierre Buf 8:42; Peca Buf 12:13; Nolan SJ 15:37

Second Period

2. San Jose, Nolan 12 (Friesen, Houlder) 6:42 (pp)
3. Buffalo, Satan 26 (Woolley, Brown) 8:28

Penalties—Sutton, SJ 2:23; Kruse Buf 6:00; Rathje SJ 10:28; Houlder SJ 16:52

Third Period

4. San Jose, Matteau 7 (Marleau, Korolyuk) 5:56
5. Buffalo, Grosek 13 (Satan, Brown) 11:22
6. Buffalo, Brown 14 (Grosek, Patrick) 16:59

Penalties—Plante Buf 3:51; San Jose (bench, unsportsmanlike conduct, served by Marleau) 16:59; Wilson Buf 19:29

Shots

San Jose	13	6	13	32
Buffalo	3	13	12	—28

Power Play—San Jose: 1-5; Buffalo: 0-6

35

St. Louis   4
at Buffalo   2

First Period

1. Buffalo, Peca 16 (Sanderson, Zhitnik) 5:04 (pp)

Penalties—Varada Buf 1:03; Campbell StL 3:30; MacInnis StL 18:12

Second Period

2. St. Louis, Pronger 8 (MacInnis, Campbell) 5:05 (pp)
3. St. Louis, Pronger 9 (MacInnis, Yake) 19:41 (pp)

Penalties—Persson StL 1:40; Sanderson Buf 2:33; Smehlik Buf 4:20; Ray Buf 6:14; Persson StL 11:37; Rasmussen Buf 15:06; Buffalo bench, served by Grosek, 18:14

Third Period

4. St. Louis, Yake 4 (Demitra) 4:59 (pp)
5. St. Louis, Eastwood 6 (Chase, Twist) 6:39
6. Buffalo, Varada 6 14:18

Penalties—Handzus StL :27; Pellerin StL 2:04; Sanderson Buf 3:06; Poeschek StL 9:38; Yake StL 11:58; Pronger StL 18:23

Shots

St. Louis	8	15	7	—30
Buffalo	8	5	12	—25

Power Play—St. Louis: 3-7; Buffalo: 1-9

36

Vancouver   4
at Colorado   4

First Period

1. Vancouver, Naslund 30 (Scatchard) 4:09 (sh)
2. Colorado, Drury 13 (Hejduk, Ozolinsh) 4:48 (pp)
3. Vancouver, Muckalt 16 (Baron) 7:33
4. Vancouver, Naslund 31 (Scatchard) 11:44 (sh)

Penalties—Gagner Van 3:21; Brashear Van 10:36

Second Period

5. Colorado, Deadmarsh 17 (Forsberg, Ozolinsh) 7:08 (pp)
6. Colorado, Forsberg 17 (Sakic, Ozolinsh) 10:19 (pp)

Penalties—Foote Col 3:08, Vancouver bench (too many men, served by Muckalt) 6:26; McCabe Van (double minor) 6:58; Kamensky Col 12:52

Third Period

7. Vancouver, Aucoin 15 (Naslund, Betuzzi) 2:07 (pp)
8. Colorado, Deadmarsh 18 (Ozolinsh, Lemieux) 7:09 (pp)

Penalties—Klemm Col 1:36; Vancouver bench (too many men, served by Washburn) 5:40; Ohlkund Van 6:50; Deadmarsh Col 7:32

Overtime

No scoring

Penalties—Muckalt Van, Gagner Van (misconduct) 2:38; Forsberg Col 3:34

Shots

Vancouver	11	8	7	1	—27
Colorado	17	15	9	2	—43

Power Play—Vancouver: 1-5; Colorado: 4-8

37
Boston 3
at Calgary 4

First Period

1. Boston, Samsonov 19 (Bourque, Allison) 7:54

Penalties—Thornton Bos (minor, major) Simpson Cal (major) 2:14; Housley Cal 13:26

Second Period

2. Calgary, Stillman 15 (Fleury, Housley) 5:02 (pp)
3. Calgary, Gauthier 1 (O'Sullivan, Stillman) 5:23
4. Boston, Allison 15 (Timander, Bourque) 14:57 (pp)

Penalties—Laaksonen Bos 3:23; Wiemer Cal 6:06; Morris Cal 14:33

Third Period

5. Calgary, Bure 12 (Stillman, Fleury) 14:19 (pp)
6. Boston, Thornton 11 (Axelsson, Bourque) 18:55
7. Calgary, Iginla 21 (Morris, Dubinsky) 19:56

Penalties—Sweeney Bos :55; Allison Bos 7:30; Shantz Cal 11:36; Ellett Bos 14:09

Shots

Boston	11	9	5	—25
Calgary	6	15	11	—32

Power Play—Boston: 1-4; Calgary 2:5

38
New Jersey 2
at Ottawa 3

First Period

1. New Jersey, McKay 11 (Brylin, Niedermayer) 14:57

Penalties—Arnott NJ 7:45; Oliwa NJ 12:01; Holik NJ 17:37; Niedermayer NJ 20:00

Second Period

2. Ottawa, Yashin 19 (York, Redden) :34 (pp)
3. New Jersey, Niedermayer 4 (McKay, Pederson) 9:03

Penalties—Brodeur NJ (served by Sharifijanov) 5:26; Salo Ott 6:58; Sharifijanov NJ 13:39; Yashin Ott 14:46; Prospal Ott 18:07

Third Period

4. Ottawa, Redden 5 (Prospal, Johansson) 2:39
5. Ottawa, Johansson 17 (Salo, Prospal) 12:47

Penalties—McKay NJ :33; Arvedson Ott 6:39; Souray NJ 14:52

Shots

New Jersey	10	11	10	—31
Ottawa	7	7	10	—24

Power Play—New Jersey: 0-4; Ottawa: 1-8

39
Washington 3
at Pittsburgh 7

First Period

1. Washington, Juneau 12 (Oates, Bondra) 7:03
2. Pittsburgh, Slegr 2 (Jagr, Miller) 11:45
3. Pittsburgh, Morozov 6 (Kesa, Titov) 15:48
4. Pittsburgh, Miller 13 (Straka, Jagr) 18:51 (pp)

Penalty—Reekie Was 17:24

Second Period

5. Pittsburgh, Titov 9 1:11 (sh)
6. Pittsburgh, Titov 10 (Barnes, Jagr) 6:17
7. Washington, Bondra 27 9:10

Penalties—Slegr Pgh:15; Klee Was 4:17; Kasparaitis Pgh 12:08; Konowalchuk Was 15:40; Pittsburgh bench (too many men, served by Miller) 19:43

Third Period

8. Washington, Oates 9 (Svejkovsky) 1:56
9. Pittsburgh, Morozov 7 (Titov, Kesa) 12:46
10. Pittsburgh, Jagr 27 (Kovalev, Straka) 15:28 (pp)

Penalties—Kasparaitis Pgh, Tabaracci Was (interference, served by Konowalchuk) 9:49; Tinordi Was 13:47; Eagles Was (major) Berube Was (misconduct) Slegr Pgh (major) 17:01; Tinordi Was 18:15

Shots

Washington	7	12	13	—32
Pittsburgh	11	6	4	—21

Power Play—Washington: 0-4; Pittsburgh: 2-5

40
Phoenix 2
at Tampa Bay 4

First Period

1. Phoenix, Tocchet 19 (Tverdovsky, Briere) 4:13
2. Tampa Bay, Clark 21 (Richer) 7:50 (pp)

Penalty—Diduck Phx (minor, game misconduct) 6:47

Second Period

No scoring

Penalties—Richer TB 5:55; Betik TB 16:02; Tucker TB 18:22

Third Period

3. Tampa Bay, Gratton 4 (McCarthy, Petrovicky) 17:15
4. Tampa Bay, Hogue 7 (Gratton, Richer) 18:28
5. Phoenix, Tocchet 20 (Roenick, Tkachuk) 19:00
6. Tampa Bay, Hogue 8 (Richer) 19:59 (en)

Penalties—Zamuner TB 1:36; Quint Phx 6:05; Cullimore TB 12:43

Shots

Phoenix	13	16	9	—39
Tampa Bay	7	8	10	—25

Power Play—Phoenix: 0-5; Tampa Bay: 1-3

Feb. 19